Caring for Your
Cat

WITHDRAWN

Susan Ring

Weigl Publishers Inc.

Project Coordinator
Diana Marshall

Design and Layout
Warren Clark
Katherine Phillips

Copy Editor
Heather Kissock

Photo Research
Gayle Murdoff

Published by Weigl Publishers Inc.
123 South Broad Street, Box 227
Mankato, MN 56002 USA
Web site: www.weigl.com

Library of Congress Cataloging-in-Publication Data

Ring, Susan.
  Caring for your cat / Susan Ring.
     v. cm. -- (Caring for your pet)
Contents: Caring for cats -- Profiles -- History -- Lifestyle -- Picking your pet -- Equipment -- What's for dinner -- Getting to know your cat -- Handling/grooming -- Keeping your cat healthy -- Behaviour -- Human interest.
  ISBN 1-59036-032-X (lib. bdg. : alk. paper)
  1. Cats--Juvenile literature. [1. Cats. 2. Pets.] I. Title. II.
Caring for your pet (Mankato, Minn.)
  SF445.7 .R55 2002
  636.8--dc21

                               2002006103

                        Printed in Canada
                 1 2 3 4 5 6 7 8 9 0   06 05 04 03 02

Photograph and Text Credits
Every reasonable effort has been made to trace ownership and to obtain permission to reprint copyright material. The publishers would be pleased to have any errors or omissions brought to their attention so that they may be corrected in subsequent printings.

Cover: kitten playing in yard (Bill Whelan/MaXx Images); **Behling and Johnson Photography:** pages 7 right, 8, 12, 13, 16, 21 top, 21 bottom, 23 bottom, 25 top; **Comstock Images:** title page, pages 5, 11 bottom, 14, 17 top, 22, 24, 28, 30; **Lorraine Hill:** page 25 bottom; **Eric Ilasenko Photo/Digital:** pages 6 middle, 26; ©**Catherine Karnow/CORBIS/MAGMA:** page 4; **Kevin King:** page 31; ©**Kevin Schafer/CORBIS/MAGMA:** page 9; **Ken Schwab/Photo Agora:** page 7 left; **Photofest:** page 6 left; **Reneé Stockdale:** pages 6 right, 7 middle, 10 top, 10 bottom, 11 top, 15 top, 15 bottom, 17 bottom, 18/19, 20, 23 top; ©**Warner Bros/Photofest:** page 27.

Kipling, Rudyard. *Just So Stories*. New York: Macmillan Education Ltd., 1983.

Contents

Cat Care

Cats are warm, furry, loving animals. For thousands of years, they have been worshiped, loved, and even feared. People are drawn to these cuddly creatures because they are beautiful and mysterious. Cats are usually very quiet. They do not require much space and do not need to be walked. A cat that jumps, plays, and chases can bring a little piece of the wild into a household.

Cats are happiest when treated gently. They will let you know if they want to be left alone.

Cats make great pets because they suit many different lifestyles.

While cats are cuddly, they are also a big responsibility. A cat requires commitment. Properly caring for cats includes giving them the things they need to stay healthy and happy. Cats need fresh water, the right foods, a warm place to sleep, and plenty of exercise. They also need to be **groomed** and taken for regular visits to the **veterinarian**.

Another important part of caring for your cat is getting to know her. Like people, each cat has a unique personality and individual needs. Take time to listen, watch, and understand these needs. When cats are cared for and loved, they return it in many ways. They can play with us, make us laugh, or comfort us when we are sad.

■ There are few things as soothing as petting a warm, soft cat as she loudly purrs.

Fascinating Facts

- About three out of every ten homes in the United States have a pet cat.
- Cats are the most common pets in the United States, followed by dogs.
- The top three most popular pet cat names in the United States are Tiger, Max, and Tigger. Sam and Kitty are also very common cat names.
- Cats purr when they are happy, sick, or in pain. Cats can purr while they inhale and exhale. Some scientists believe that purring is caused by a vibration of vocal cords. Others believe that it is caused by air moving through the blood vessels.

Pet Profiles

Cats are different sizes, shapes, and colors. Most house cats are mixed-breed cats. This means they are a mixture of different cat **breeds**. Some people prefer **purebred** cats. There are about 40 cat breeds, many with distinct features. The Turkish Van has waterproof fur. The Manx does not have a tail.

SPHINX

- No hair or whiskers at all
- Wrinkled skin
- The first Sphinx was born in 1966 to two furry parents
- Loves to be watched
- Does not enjoy being the only pet in a household, so it is best to own another cat or even a dog

DOMESTIC

- One of the most common types of house cat
- General name that includes all **nonpedigreed** cats
- Variety of colors, sizes, markings, and shapes
- Includes long-haired and short-haired
- Variety of temperaments

RAGDOLL

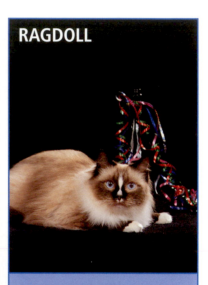

- Large, fluffy body with long, silky coat
- Light-colored fur with darker areas around the face, legs, tail, and ears
- Grooms often
- Requires much combing and brushing
- Very loving
- Laid-back personality
- Gentle with children
- Is a floor cat; not a jumper

Cats are also divided into a large variety of coat colorings and markings. Calico cats' coats are always **tricolored**. The tabby cat's name describes the markings, or patterns, on its coat. Tabby markings include dark lines around the eyes, dark whisker tips, and an M-shaped pattern on the forehead.

SIAMESE

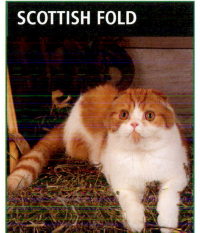

- Very intelligent
- Very vocal; will meow loudly and often
- Short hair
- Sleek, tan body with dark paws, tail, ears, and head
- Large, pointed ears
- Thin, pointed head
- Strong, independent, self-assured personality
- Requires much attention

SCOTTISH FOLD

- Born with straight ears, but at about 3 weeks old, ears fold over forward
- Long or short hair
- Variety of colors
- Sweet and loving
- Quickly adapts to change and any environment

PERSIAN

- Most popular breed in the world
- Very long, fluffy coat
- Requires a great deal of daily grooming, combing, and brushing
- Variety of colors
- Flat face and stocky body
- Quiet and loving

From Wild to Mild

Cats have lived on Earth for millions of years. Scientists have found ancient **fossils** of the first ancestor of many of today's big cats, including the lion. Called *Miacis,* this weasel-like animal is believed to have been the ancestor of present-day **domestic** cats as well. The fossils reveal that *Miacis* lived about 50 million years ago. It took thousands of years for the wildcats of the past to become today's domestic cats.

If your pet is an outdoor cat, be prepared to receive gifts of the hunt, such as dead birds and mice.

■ Members of the cat family first appeared about 40 million years ago.

African wildcats are likely the closest relatives to present-day house cats. African wildcats were domesticated by the ancient Egyptians as early as 2500 BC. These wildcats would come to people's homes to kill mice for food. The mice ate people's grain, so the Egyptians enjoyed having the cats around. People began to feed and care for the cats that were the most friendly.

◼ African wildcats can still be found in various parts of Africa.

Fascinating Facts

- Experts believe that cats and humans have shared their homes for about 5,000 years.
- The Egyptian cat goddess, Bastet, had the body of a woman and the head of a cat. She was the goddess of love and fertility.
- When cats died in ancient Egypt, they were **mummified** and buried with their owners.

Life Cycle

It is fun to play with a cute, tiny kitten. It is equally important to spend time with older, adult cats. Throughout their lifetime, cats depend on their owners. From a newborn kitten to a senior cat, your pet's needs will change during her lifetime.

Newborn Kitten

Kittens are born completely helpless. Their eyes are closed and will not open for 8 to 12 days. They cannot walk very well. Instead, kittens crawl. Most of their time is spent sleeping and drinking their mother's milk. Always wash your hands before handling a newborn kitten. Germs on your hands can make a newborn kitten sick.

More than Ten Years

As they get older, cats begin to need more sleep. They are less active. Their hearing and eyesight may begin to fail. Senior cats may still be playful. They may require a special diet, as some foods are hard to digest. Extra nutrients may also be needed.

Fascinating Facts

- The average life span of a cat is about 16 years. In 1939 in England, a cat named Puss died at 36 years of age.
- Female cats usually give birth to four kittens at a time.

Four Weeks

At 4 weeks old, kittens are alert and walking. They are very curious. They explore and discover new things. They still spend much of their day sleeping. They are more independent, but will watch their mother to learn how to groom and use the litter box. Four-week-old kittens love to chase balls, strings, or ribbons.

One Year

Cats are fully grown at 1 year of age. They are independent and spend more time alone. Still, they will rely on you for their health and happiness. One-year-old cats need help staying fit and energetic. Pet owners should keep plenty of toys around the house.

Picking Your Pet

There are many factors to consider and research before selecting a pet. These factors will help you choose the best pet to be your furry friend. There are some important questions to think about before picking your pet.

Kittens should not be taken from their mother until they are 12 weeks old.

What Will a Cat Cost?

Many cats in city shelters are just waiting for a good home. These are often cats that have been rescued off the street. Pet stores sell many types of kittens. They cost more than cats from shelters, but will include some basic supplies and the cat will be **vaccinated**. A purebred cat will be the most expensive option. When calculating the cost of buying a cat, be sure to include the costs of toys, food, bedding, and litter.

Kittens for Adoption

■ Cats from shelters are usually cheap. Sometimes, they are even free.

Will a new cat get along with your other pets?

What Do I Have Time For?

Do you have time to spend with an active, frisky kitten? You may prefer an adult cat, as they require less attention. Long-haired cats must be brushed and groomed at least once a day. Short-haired cats need less grooming. No matter what your cat looks like or how old he is, you will have to feed him, groom him, and clean his litter box every day.

How Will a Cat Affect my Family?

It is very important to find out if anyone in your family has allergies. Bringing a cat into the home may be dangerous for an allergic sister or brother. Think about other pets you already have at home. How will the family dog or hamster be affected by a new cat?

Fascinating Facts

- Every year, Americans spend more than $4 billion on cat food.
- Scientific studies reveal that people who own cats live longer, have fewer heart attacks, and suffer from less stress.
- Many plants are toxic to cats. Preparing for a new cat includes cat-proofing your home. Remove poisonous plants, such as tiger lilies, daffodils, and mistletoe.

Cat Supplies

Before bringing a cat home, you will need a few basic supplies. These include food and water dishes, a litter box, and a comfortable bed. While you may choose to bring your cat home in a cardboard pet box, you can also buy a cat carrier in advance. A large, sturdy carrier can double as a bed. To protect your furniture, your cat should have a scratching post on which to sharpen her claws. A very young kitten may need a warm hot-water bottle and a ticking clock in his bed. These will help him feel less lonely. Toys are very important to keep your cat active and alert.

Put your new cat in one room for a few days. This will help him slowly adjust to his new home.

■ Most cats do not like car trips. A cat carrier can help you transport your frightened pet to the veterinarian.

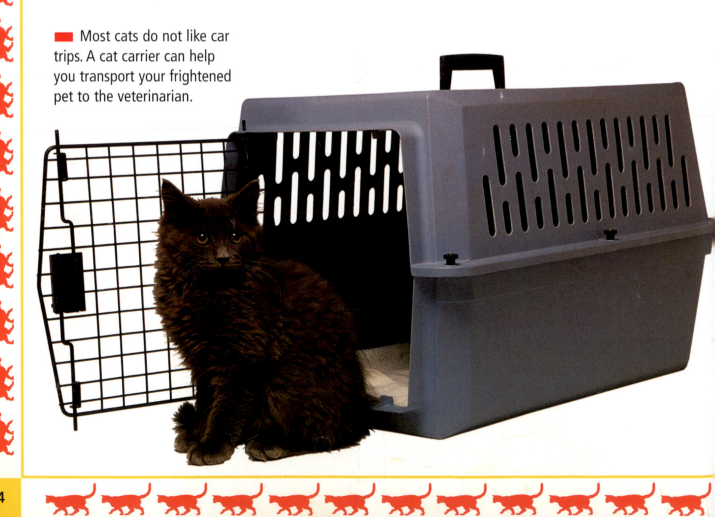

The litter box should be at least 12 inches wide, 16 inches long, and 3.5 inches deep.

Both indoor and outdoor cats need a litter box inside the house. It can be covered or open. The litter box should always be placed away from the cat's bed, and food and water dishes.

Cat beds can be bought at pet supplies stores. Many cats are happy sleeping in a cardboard box lined with blankets. The bed should be placed in a warm room, away from drafts. Do not be surprised if your cat ignores the bed you offer her and chooses her own sleeping arrangements. Often, cats need to feel that they have a special spot in the house that is their own.

Cleanliness is important to cats. Once you know your cat's fur type and length, you may buy a brush and comb for grooming.

Fascinating Facts

- Some cats can be trained to go to the bathroom directly into the toilet. These cats do not use a litter box at all.

Feeding a Feline

Cats are fussy eaters. It is important to vary your cat's foods. Otherwise, she may develop a taste for one food so much that she will refuse to eat anything else. Canned food is available in many flavors and can give your cat all the vitamins she needs. Dry food should also be given. It cleans and strengthens cats' teeth. Most people feed their cats half canned and half dry food for a healthy balance. You may also want to feed your cat fresh food occasionally. Cats love cooked chicken or turkey. If you feed your cat fresh fish, be sure to remove all the bones. Your cat's water dish should always be fresh and full.

Never feed your cat dog food. It does not contain enough protein to fulfill your cat's dietary needs.

■ Cats are carnivores. This means that their diet consists mainly of meat and fish.

How Much Food?

The labels on cat food include feeding instructions. Still, you should be aware of what works best for your cat. If your cat never finishes the food in his bowl, consider giving smaller portions. If your cat gains weight, try feeding him less often. Veterinarians recommend that cats be fed twice a day.

Treats make most cats happy. These foods come in all shapes, sizes, and flavors. Since most treats offer little nutritional value, they should not be given too often.

■ Since most cats stop eating when they are full, leftover food should be taken away to prevent it from spoiling.

Fascinating Facts

- Cats need fat in their diet because their bodies cannot produce it on their own.
- Cats need five times more protein than dogs.
- Chocolate is poisonous to cats.
- Most cats prefer their food at room temperature.
- To drink, a cat laps liquid from the underside of his tongue.

Fast and Furry

Whether a simple alley cat or a majestic lion, all cats have certain features in common. Most cats have fur on their bodies to keep them warm. Cats are fast, **agile**, strong, and smart. Their senses are keen and sensitive. These characteristics help make the cat a great hunter.

Very strong back legs help cats jump onto high surfaces. Cats, along with camels and giraffes, walk by moving both their left legs, then both their right legs. This helps them walk silently and quickly.

A cat's tail is an extension of its backbone. Cats use their tail for balance and to show their moods.

Since cats are **predators**, they need to run quickly. Domestic cats can run about 30 miles per hour. Cats also have sharp **retractable** claws. The bottoms of their paws are protected by tough pads.

■ TABBY

Cats have very keen hearing. They can move their ears to locate sounds. Each ear can be moved independently and can turn 180 degrees.

Cats can see in the dark about six times better than humans. A cat's pupils grow very large and round in low light. This allows more light to enter. In bright light, a cat's pupils become narrow slits.

Even before they can see, kittens use their sharp sense of smell to guide them. A cat's nose can tell him who or what has been in a room before him.

A cat's whiskers are extremely sensitive to touch. Whiskers help cats feel their way through small spaces and dim light. A cat can judge whether his body will fit in a tight space by whether his whiskers fit.

A cat's mouth contains sharp, pointed, front teeth that are used for grabbing and ripping meat. Their rough tongue helps them groom and drink.

Purr-fect Grooming

Cats spend much of their time grooming and cleaning themselves. They lick a paw and, using it like a washcloth, clean their face. Their rough tongues act like combs, pulling out dirt and twigs. Still, sharing the grooming between cat and owner is very important. Grooming helps a kitten adjust to being handled. It also helps owners check their cat's fur and skin to make sure they are healthy. Regular grooming creates a bond between cat and owner. Most cats purr when they are being brushed.

Regular grooming helps prevent hairballs. When grooming themselves, cats can swallow too much fur. This fur can block their stomachs.

Long-haired cats must be brushed every day to prevent tangles and knots.

■ The sooner you begin brushing your cat, the more likely she is to enjoy being groomed.

It is important to use the right brush for your cat's fur type. Different fur types and lengths need different kinds of brushes. Once you have found the right brush for your cat, you are ready to begin. Hold the cat on your lap or in front of you on the floor. Slowly look through your cat's fur. Check for **mats**, burrs, and skin sores. Gently brush downward from the head to the tail. After brushing, long-haired cats should be combed with a wide-toothed comb.

Cats' claws must be regularly trimmed. They must be clipped at a certain spot on the claw. This must be done carefully. Ask a veterinarian to show you how to cut your cat's claws before you try it on your own.

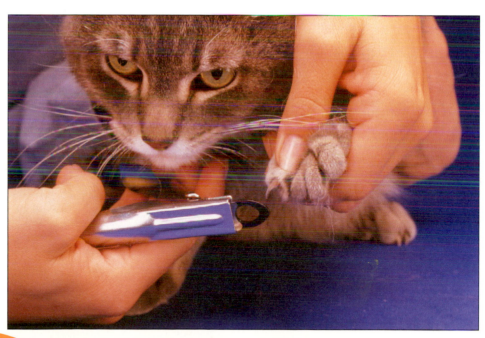

Small claw clippers are made specifically for cat-sized claws.

Fascinating Facts

- Cats do not need baths. Most cats do not like water. Only when cats have fleas will they need to be bathed and shampooed.
- Scratching is a natural instinct for cats. As long as they have claws, they will scratch. Many veterinarians oppose declawing. Cats' claws are part of the toe bone. The operation that removes the claw also removes the last joint of each toe. It is painful because it changes the form of the paw. It also changes the way the cat walks and runs.

Healthy and Happy

A healthy cat is a happy cat. Grooming and the right foods will keep your cat healthy. Loving and caring for your cat does a great deal to keep her happy. Regular exercise helps your cat stay fit.

Choose a veterinarian that makes you feel at ease. Your veterinarian will answer questions about your cat's behavior and health. The veterinarian can also give your cat vaccines. These will protect her from common cat illnesses. Talk to your veterinarian about **neutering** or **spaying** your cat. This operation prevents male cats from fighting and **spraying**, and prevents female cats from having kittens.

Never give aspirin to a cat. Cats can die from eating aspirin or other human medicines.

■ Take your cat to the veterinarian at least once a year for a checkup.

Once you know your cat's personality, it will be easier to notice when something is wrong. Take note of pattern changes. Is your cat sleeping more or eating less? Have her bathroom habits changed? Is she drinking more water than usual? A cat is likely sick if she is coughing or sneezing. Be aware of limping or licking of wounds. These may need veterinary care.

Cats are playful and curious. Sometimes, they can get into trouble and hurt themselves. Take some time to make sure your home is safe for your cat.

■ Keep such items as pins, needles, plastic bags, wires, and garbage out of your cat's reach. Cats may choke on them or eat something that could make them very ill.

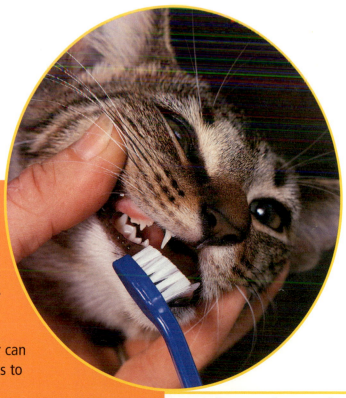

Fascinating Facts

- Cats can develop gum disease and tooth decay. They should have their teeth cleaned by a veterinarian once a year. Special cat toothbrushes and toothpastes also keep your cat's mouth healthy.
- Cats with white and light-colored fur can get a sunburn. It is best for these cats to stay out of the sun.

Cat Behavior

Even though cats are very independent, they still enjoy bonding and playing with their owner. Indoor cats need more toys and activities than cats that adventure outdoors. All cats need plenty of love and attention.

Cats are smart. They can be trained and disciplined. Sometimes cats can be naughty. Bad behavior can be gently corrected with a firm "no." A cat should never be hit. A hug or a treat can be given to reward your cat when he has done something good.

A cat's senses are alert, even during naps. Poking or pulling a sleeping cat's tail may result in a scratch.

■ Cats are almost always in the mood to chase a toy, bat a ball, or play hide-and-seek in a paper bag.

Pet Peeves

Cats do not like:
• loud noises
• barking dogs
• too much attention
• too little attention
• closed doors
• being moved from a warm lap when sleeping
• having their tails pulled

Cats spend almost one-third of their day grooming themselves.

Even though your cat cannot speak, he can communicate with you in other ways. Your cat will let you know when he is happy, upset, or afraid by the movement of his tail. A loud purr usually means he is content. Cats that are grooming usually want to be alone. When a cat rubs his head against you, he is looking for attention. Cats rub their heads against people or objects. This marks the person or object with the scent glands found between the cat's eye and ear. Your cat will be more comfortable when he recognizes his scent on you. With time, patience, and close attention, you will learn to understand what your cat is saying to you when he meows, purrs, licks, chirps, and hisses.

Fascinating Facts

- Some cats go crazy over **catnip**. About 80 percent of cats respond to the herb by drooling, rubbing, purring, and rolling around.
- When cats are afraid, they often jump to a higher place in the room. Heights allow them to see much more. This makes them feel more secure.
- The sleepiest of all mammals, cats spend 16 hours of each day sleeping.

Cat Tales

President Theodore Roosevelt had a gray cat named Slippers. Slippers had six toes on each foot. Slippers would disappear for days but always returned for large state dinners at the White House. He sat wherever he wished, and visitors at the White House had to walk around him.

From presidents to movie stars, many important people have been pet cat lovers. Famous friends to felines include Daniel Boone, the legendary American frontiersman; Sir Isaac Newton, who discovered the theory of gravity and invented the first cat-flap door; Mark Twain, the author of *The Adventures of Huckleberry Finn;* and U.S. presidents Abraham Lincoln and George Washington.

Fascinating Facts

- About 95 percent of pet cat owners admit that they regularly talk to their cat.
- During his time as the governor of California, Ronald Reagan signed a bill that made it illegal to kick cats.
- In 1950, a 4-month-old kitten in Switzerland followed mountain climbers all the way to the top of the 14,691-foot Matterhorn, in the Swiss Alps.

From famous cat owners to celebrity cats, these furry creatures have appeared in books, movies, television shows, stories, and fables. Sylvester and Tweety first appeared together in "Tweety Pie," in 1947. This television episode earned the Warner Brothers cartoon department its first Academy Award. Sylvester was a kitty with a killer instinct. Audiences watched Sylvester chase his feathered enemy in more than 40 cartoons.

■ Sylvester showed that even house cats have the hunting instinct.

Of Cats and Men

"The Cat that Walked by Himself" is a fable that explains the personality of the domestic cat. The cat may have become a tame companion, but he still maintains an independent spirit. In this fable, the dog, the horse, and the cow agree to become domesticated. The cat still resists, longing for his wild life. The cat appears at the human's den and says, "I am not a friend, and I am not a servant. I am the cat who walks by himself, and I wish to come into your cave." A deal is made between cats and men. The cat promises to catch mice forever, as long as he is allowed to walk by himself.

From Rudyard Kipling's *Just So Stories*.

Pet Puzzlers

What do you know about cats? If you can answer the following questions correctly, you may be ready to own a cat.

Q What does a cat use her whiskers for?

A cat uses her whiskers to determine whether her body will fit in a narrow space.

Q Why are cat toys so important?

A domestic cat still has many of the instincts of the wild. Your pet cat may become restless or depressed if he is bored and inactive. It is important to keep your cat strong, healthy, and energetic with a variety of toys and games.

Q Why must long-haired cats be brushed daily?

Long-haired cats need to be groomed at least once a day. This prevents tangles, knots, and mats that can be painful and annoying to a cat. Regular brushing also combats hairballs.

Q How often should you feed your cat?

It is recommended that cats be fed twice a day. The quantity of food may vary depending on your cat's particular appetite. Half of their meal should be canned food, while the rest should be dry food.

Q How do cats communicate with their owners?

Purring, wagging tails, meowing, and rubbing against their owner's legs are some of the ways that cats tell humans how they are feeling.

Q How long have cats been domesticated?

Experts believe that cats and humans have lived together for about 5,000 years.

Q When should you have your cat neutered or spayed?

Veterinarians agree that cats should undergo this operation at 6 months of age.

Calling Your Cat

Before you buy your pet cat, write down some cat names you like. Some names may work better for a female cat. Others may suit a male cat. Here are just a few suggestions:

Fluffy

Sylvester

Ginger

Smokey

Socks

Sheba

Snuggles

Garfield

Puss

Morris

Frequently Asked Questions

Should I give my cat extra vitamins?

Cats that eat good, balanced, nutritious cat food do not need extra nutrients. Some cat owners give vitamins to cats who are pregnant, very old, or under stress. Vitamins should always be given following the advice of a veterinarian.

How can I keep my cat cool in the summer?

Cats are good at keeping themselves cool in hot weather. Remember that cats always need to have fresh water available. It may help to keep the blinds closed during the day to block sunlight. A fan blowing in the room can help as well.

Why does my cat scratch the furniture?

Cats need to sharpen their claws. This prevents their claws from growing too long and hurting their paws. While outdoor cats will use trees, indoor cats need a scratching post. Little caps that fit over each claw can also protect your cat, as well as your furniture. Talk to your veterinarian about ways you can work with your cat to help him change this behavior.

More Information

Animal Organizations

You can help cats stay healthy and happy by learning more about them. Many organizations are dedicated to teaching people how to care for and protect their pet pals. For more cat information, write to the following organizations:

American Cat Association
8101 Katherine Avenue
Panorama City, CA 91402

Humane Society of the United States
2100 L Street N.W.
Washington, DC 20037

Web Sites

To answer more of your cat questions, go online and surf to the following Web sites:

Care for Animals
www.avma.org/careforanimals/
animatedjourneys/animatedfl.asp

Cat Health and Kitten Care
www.cat-health-and-kitten-care.com/

Humane Society of the United States
www.hsus.org

Words to Know

agile: athletic; moves easily

breeds: groups of animals that share specific characteristics

catnip: a plant with sweet-smelling oils

domestic: tamed and used to living among people

fossils: remains of animals and plants from long ago found in rocks

groomed: cleaned by removing dirt from fur

mats: tangles, knots, and clumps of fur

mummified: preserved dead body

neutering: making male animals unable to reproduce

nonpedigreed: not having a pure line of ancestors

predators: animals that hunt and kill other animals for food

purebred: animals whose relatives are known and in whom the same traits have been passed on through the generations

retractable: able to withdraw

spaying: making female animals unable to reproduce

spraying: marking territory with urine

tricolored: three colors; calico cats are usually orange, black, and white

vaccinated: injected with medicines that help prevent certain diseases or illnesses

veterinarian: animal doctor

Index

6|06

CLEOPATRA

Other titles in the
RVLERS OF THE ANCIENT WORLD series:

ALEXANDER THE GREAT
**Conqueror of
the Ancient World**
0-7660-2560-8

HANNIBAL
**Great General
of the Ancient World**
0-7660-2564-0

JULIUS CAESAR
**Ruler of
the Roman World**
0-7660-2563-2

PERICLES
**Great Leader
of Ancient Athens**
0-7660-2561-6

RAMESSES II
Ruler of Ancient Egypt
0-7660-2562-4

CLEOPATRA

Queen of Ancient Egypt

Richard Worth

Enslow Publishers, Inc.

40 Industrial Road   PO Box 38
Box 398   Aldershot
Berkeley Heights, NJ 07922   Hants GU12 6BP
USA   UK

http://www.enslow.com

Library of Congress Cataloging-in-Publication Data

Worth, Richard.
    Cleopatra : queen of ancient Egypt / by Richard Worth.
        p. cm. — (Rulers of the ancient world)
    Includes bibliographical references and index.
    ISBN 0-7660-2559-4
    1. Cleopatra, Queen of Egypt, d. 30 B.C.—Juvenile literature. 2. Egypt—History—332–30
B.C.—Juvenile literature. 3. Queens—Egypt—Biography—Juvenile literature. I. Title.
II. Series.
    DT92.7.W67   2005
    932'.021'092—dc22

                             2005004190

Printed in the United States of America

10 9 8 7 6 5 4 3 2 1

To Our Readers:
We have done our best to make sure that all Internet addresses in this book were active and
appropriate when we went to press. However, the author and publisher have no control over and
assume no liability for the material available on those Internet sites or on other Web sites they may
link to. Any comments or suggestions can be sent by e-mail to comments@enslow.com or to the
address on the back cover.

Illustration Credits: Ancient Art & Architecture Collection Ltd ©AAAC / Topham / The Image
Works, p. 3; © The British Museum/HIP/The Image Works, p. 72; Clipart.com, pp. 18 (top), 57, 93,
97; © Corel Corporation, pp. 24 (background), 37, 134, 140; Enslow Publishers, Inc., pp. 14, 18
(bottom), 24, 27, 40, 109; Gian Luigi Scarfiotti/*Saudi Aramco World*/PADIA, p. 41; John
Feeney/*Saudi Aramco World*/PADIA, pp. 44, 91; Michael Grimsdale/*Saudi Aramco World*/PADIA,
٦. 16, 26; Reproduced from the Collections of the Library of Congress, pp. 8, 75, 116, 123;
ɔroduced from *Egyptian Designs* published by Dover Publications, Inc., pp. 48, 67, 79.

    ead and Chapter Opener Illustrations: Reproduced from *Egyptian Designs* published by
· Publications, Inc.

    ʼlustration: Ancient Art & Architecture Collection Ltd ©AAAC / Topham / The Image

To my dear friend, Karen Jeffers.

Acknowledgments

I wish to thank Professor Gene Wood Davis,
my ancient history teacher at Trinity College.

CONTENTS

Cleopatra (on left) was the last ruler of ancient Egypt. This carving of the great queen appears on the side of the Temple of Hathor in Egypt.

TRIUMPH

As the Roman legions entered the city of Alexandria in 48 B.C., Cleopatra, ruler of Egypt, faced two difficult problems. She was waging a civil war against her brother, Ptolemy, for Egypt's throne and control of the entire country. Ptolemy had taken control of the capital and driven Cleopatra out of the city.

Julius Caesar led the Roman legions. Rome had the most powerful army in the Mediterranean world, and Caesar was Rome's greatest general. Cleopatra needed his help to regain her throne. At the same time, she wanted to retain Egypt's independence in the face of Rome's powerful army. While gaining Caesar as an ally, she did not want Egypt to become the slave of Rome.

THE ARRIVAL OF CLEOPATRA

Caesar sent a messenger to Cleopatra, summoning her to the palace in Alexandria. At first, she sent only ambassadors. Cleopatra did not want to expose herself to Ptolemy's army, which controlled Alexandria. She eventually decided to come in person. The Roman historian Cassius Dio thought that Cleopatra believed that she could charm Caesar and persuade him to let her retake the throne.[1] Somehow, Cleopatra's ship managed to slip past Ptolemy's navy into the harbor at Alexandria. Then a friend, named Apollodorus, brought her in a small boat to the shore near the palace. As the ancient historian Plutarch wrote, "She was at a loss how to get in undiscovered, till she thought of putting herself into the coverlet of a bed and lying at length, whilst Apollodorus tied up the bedding and carried it on his back through the gates to Caesar's apartment."[2]

Was this story true? Modern historians have found no evidence to contradict the words of Plutarch. However, he wrote his history more than a century after Cleopatra's death. Indeed, historian Ernle Bradford praises Cleopatra for her

> incredible courage in venturing right into the heartland of her enemies. . . . her brother, and all his court were determined on her death, while the Romans and even Caesar himself might, for all she knew, have been brought over to their side. . . . What Caesar will have appreciated above all was that here—like himself—was another real gambler.[3]

As a victorious general, Julius Caesar had been forced to take many risks in battle. These risks had paid off in great military victories.

As he began to talk with the queen, Caesar was also attracted to her intelligence. He had met many other noble women and monarchs in his military campaigns, but Cleopatra apparently stood out as being very unusual. Did her beauty also captivate him? Plutarch wrote:

> For her actual beauty, it is said, was not in itself so remarkable that none could be compared with her, or

that no one could see her without being struck by it, but the contact of her presence, if you lived with her, was irresistible; the attraction of her person, joining with the charm of her conversation, and the character that attended all she said or did, was something bewitching. It was a pleasure merely to hear the sound of her voice, with which, like an instrument of many strings, she could pass from one language to another.[4]

Historians have disagreed about Cleopatra's appearance. Writing after Plutarch, Cassius Dio said: ". . . she was a woman of surpassing beauty, and at that time [when she met Caesar], she was in the prime of her youth, she was most striking; she also possessed a charming voice and a knowledge of how to make herself agreeable to every one."[5] Coins from the period of Cleopatra's reign, however, paint a different picture. They show a thin woman, with a somewhat large, hooked nose and thin lips.

Whatever her appearance, Cleopatra made the best of it. Egyptian men and women regularly used makeup to highlight their faces. Makeup for a woman like Cleopatra included blackening for her eyebrows and for lining her eyelids. The queen probably used ocher—a mixture of iron and clay that created an orange or gray pigment—as a kind of lipstick. The queen used plant juices in rouge for her cheeks.

There is no doubt that Caesar was attracted to the twenty-year-old Cleopatra. Historians agree that the fifty-three-year-old Caesar began a romantic relationship with her. Cleopatra hoped to use her powers to exercise some control over Caesar. The queen believed that

Rome could safeguard Egypt's independence. But she also wanted something more. By allying herself with Caesar and using her charms on him, she wanted to restore some of Egypt's former glory and power.[6] Centuries earlier, Egypt had been a great power. But in the first century B.C., Egypt was considered a second-rate power compared to Rome. Finally, Cleopatra needed Caesar's help to achieve something else. She wanted to rule Egypt as the queen without any interference from her brother, Ptolemy.

With her charm, her intelligence, and her political skills, Cleopatra achieved all of these goals. She also became Egypt's most famous monarch.

CHILDHOOD

Cleopatra was born in 69 B.C. in Alexandria, Egypt. Her name, which is Greek, means "her father's glory." Cleopatra's father was the pharaoh Ptolemy XII. He was called Auletes, which means flute player in Greek. Ptolemy was a talented musician.

When Cleopatra was born, Alexandria was the largest city in the Mediterranean area. It was a splendid metropolis with a population of about five hundred thousand people. The city had been founded in 331 B.C. by the Macedonian Greek leader Alexander the Great. He had conquered much of the known world, including the Egyptian civilization.

Cleopatra grew up in the northeastern section of Alexandria, called the Bruchion. She lived in the royal palace there. Greek pharaohs named Ptolemy had ruled Egypt for almost three centuries. Many of their queens had also been called Cleopatra.

As she grew up, Cleopatra learned about the conquests of Alexander. He was considered a military genius. In his early twenties, Alexander led an army out of Greece against the mighty Persian Empire. This war had been planned by Alexander's father, Philip of Macedon, before his death. The Greeks invaded the Persian Empire in 334 B.C. This empire stretched across

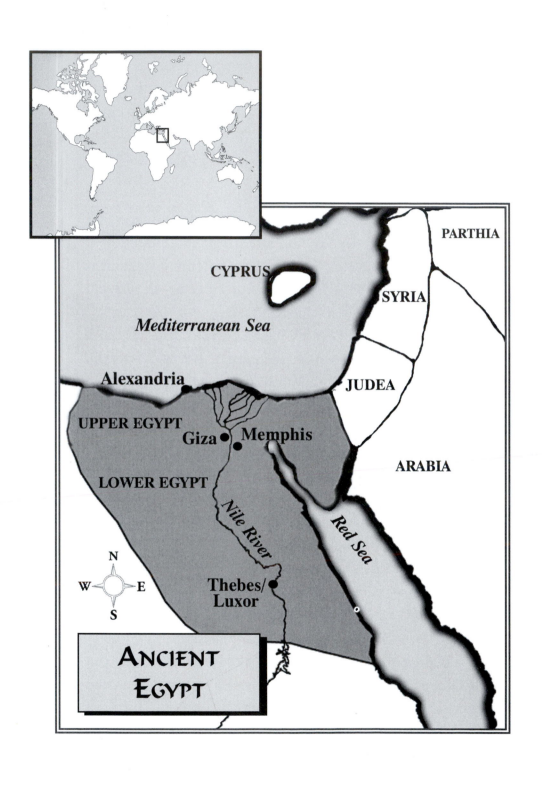

CYPRUS

Mediterranean Sea

PARTHIA

SYRIA

JUDEA

ARABIA

Alexandria

UPPER EGYPT

Giza ● Memphis

LOWER EGYPT

Nile River

Red Sea

N
W ✦ E
S

Thebes/
Luxor

ANCIENT
EGYPT

Asia Minor, through the present-day Middle East, and south into Egypt. Over the next several years, Alexander defeated the Persians in a series of battles. Eventually, he conquered all the territories ruled by the Persians. He controlled what are modern-day Egypt, Iran, and Afghanistan and even marched into northern India. But at the age of only thirty-one, Alexander died of a mysterious illness in Babylon (located in the present-day country of Iraq).

THE FIRST PHARAOH NAMED PTOLEMY

After Alexander's death, his vast empire was divided. One of Alexander's generals, a cousin named Ptolemy, claimed Egypt. Ptolemy's father was named Lagos. Therefore, his family is known as the Lagides. They are also called the Ptolemies. Ptolemy marched south and took control of Egypt. Ptolemy also brought Alexander's body with him. Ptolemy built a giant mausoleum, or tomb, for Alexander. He began referring to Alexander as a young god. This appealed to many Egyptians, who had long considered their pharaohs to be gods.

Ptolemy I (304–282) was called Soter, meaning savior. He regarded himself as the man who had saved Egypt from other rulers who wanted to control it. A brilliant civilization had existed in Egypt for more than three thousand years. The Egyptian pharaohs had built great temples and magnificent pyramids. However, Egypt was eventually conquered by a series of stronger rulers. They included Ptolemy Soter.

Ptolemy established his new capital at Alexandria. This city was located at one of the mouths of the Nile River, where it poured into the Mediterranean Sea. At this point, the Nile deposits mud and soil, forming a large delta. Ptolemy laid out a magnificent city at the delta. It was praised by the Greek geographer Strabo, who lived during the same period as Cleopatra. "The whole city," he said, "is crossed by streets wide enough for horses and carriages. . . . The city has magnificent public places and buildings and royal palaces that cover a quarter, even a third, of the total city area."[1]

The city was laid out like a giant grid, 3.75 miles long and one mile wide. It was eventually divided into five sections. Jews, Greeks, Egyptians, and foreign soldiers

This drawing shows the Alexandria of Cleopatra's time. In the background is the harbor and the Great Lighthouse, which later became one of the seven wonders of the Ancient World.

lived in different sections of the city. Canals brought water into Alexandria from the Nile River. At one end of the city was Lake Mareotis, which was also linked to the Nile by a canal. At the entrance to Alexandria lay Pharos Island. A long causeway, called the Heptastadion, connected the city to Pharos Island. This causeway divided the entrance to Alexandria into two parts. These dual harbors protected ships from great storms. If a storm came from one direction toward one of the harbors, ships could move to the second harbor on the other side of the causeway for protection.

In his magnificent capital, Ptolemy I began to plan beautiful buildings like those he had seen in Greece. There were magnificent temples to the gods and goddesses. There was a large outdoor theater for staging Greek plays. There was also an open square, called an agora. The Greeks built a gymnasium, a large building where Greek men competed in sports and enjoyed physical exercise. They were also taught by Greek tutors, men who were experts in philosophy, public speaking, and mathematics. Strabo wrote, "The gymnasium is the most beautiful building, with a colonnade about 175 metres [approximately 575 feet] in length. In the middle of the city are the law courts and open groves."[2]

Ptolemy I built a center devoted only to learning. This was called the Museum, the place of the Muses. These were Greek goddesses who inspired poets, writers, and thinkers. Ptolemy brought Greek thinkers to work at the Museum. Later, after his death, scientists and mathematicians also came there to develop their ideas.

Great Scientists at Alexandria

The Museum of Alexandria brought together some of the greatest minds of the ancient world. Among them was Euclid (325 B.C.–265 B.C.), author of a book called *The Elements*. This book became a standard mathematics textbook for more than two thousand  years. It presents and proves the major principles of geometry. For example, Euclid proved that a straight line can be drawn between any two points. He also proved that all right angles are equal.

Another scientist who worked at the museum was Archimedes (287 B.C.–212 B.C.) Born in Syracuse on the island of Sicily, Archimedes traveled to Alexandria when he was still young. A brilliant mathematician, he developed the Archimedes screw, which is placed inside  a cylinder to create a pump. When the bottom of the cylinder is placed in water and the screw is turned, water is raised. This pump has been used for centuries to drain farmlands and also to provide water for irrigating fields.

A third great thinker who worked at Alexandria was Eratosthenes (276 B.C.–194 B.C.). Born in Cyrene in present-day Libya, Eratosthenes became chief librarian of the Museum of Alexandria about 240 B.C. He made enormous contributions to geography. These included measuring the diameter of the earth. Eratosthenes calculated the distance to the moon, and drew the location and route of the Nile River. He also thought that the earth was round.

As a young girl, Cleopatra was educated by some of the Greeks who worked at the Museum. She learned Greek philosophy and studied the works of Greek poets, like Homer. The poet Homer had composed an epic poem of the ancient city of Troy, located in Asia Minor. Known as the *Iliad*, this long or epic poem described the Trojan War. This war was probably fought about 1200 B.C. Homer also wrote the *Odyssey,* about a hero returning home from the Trojan War. Cleopatra also studied music and mathematics. In addition, she became a highly skilled linguist. Cleopatra mastered many of the languages spoken by people across the Mediterranean world. This helped her when she eventually became Queen of Egypt. Cleopatra became very popular with the Egyptians because she could speak their language. She was also able to converse with the leaders of other civilizations. As the Greek historian Plutarch wrote:

> There were few of the barbarian nations that she answered by an interpreter; to most of them she spoke herself, as to the Ethiopians . . . Hebrews, Arabians, Syrians . . . and many others, whose language she had learnt; which was all the more surprising because most of the kings, her predecessors, [the Ptolemies] scarcely gave themselves the trouble to acquire the Egyptian tongue. [3]

PTOLEMY II AND THE GROWTH OF THE EMPIRE

Ptolemy I was followed by his son Ptolemy (282 B.C.– 246 B.C.). He was called Philadelphus, which means "lover of a brother or sister." More than a thousand

A Great Parade

When Philidelphus became king of Egypt, there was a great parade held for him. Below, part of the parade is described. It was the portion of the parade that honored the Greek god Dionysus.

Next came boys in purple tunics, bearing frankincense and myrrh, and saffron on golden dishes. And then advanced forty Satyrs, crowned with golden ivy garlands; their bodies were painted some with purple, some with vermilion, and some with other colors. They wore each a golden crown, made to imitate vine leaves and ivy leaves. Presently also came Philiscus the Poet, who was a priest of Dionysus, and with him all the artisans employed in the service of that god; . . .

The next-was a four-wheeled wagon . . . drawn by one hundred and eighty men. On it was an image of Dionysus. . . . He was pouring libations from a golden goblet, and had a purple tunic reaching to his feet. . . . In front of him lay a Lacedaemonian goblet of gold, holding fifteen measures of wine, and a golden tripod, in which was a golden incense burner, and two golden bowls full of cassia and saffron; and a shade covered it round adorned with ivy and vine leaves, and all other kinds of greenery.[4]

years earlier, the Egyptian pharaohs had married their sisters. The pharaoh was thought by Egyptians to be the god Osiris. Egyptians believed that Osiris had married his sister, the goddess Isis. She had a child, named Horus. Egyptian pharaohs followed the traditions of their gods. Ptolemy Philadelphus called himself a god and decided to carry out the same traditions as the early Egyptian pharaohs. This was an effort by Philadelphus to combine Egyptian traditions with those of the new Greek monarchy.

The Egyptians had a religious tradition that was centuries old. Religious temples throughout Egypt were maintained by priests who shaved their heads and wore white linen robes. Priests, men as well as women, were selected by the Pharaohs. They had to pay a tax to the Egyptian government to become priests. But they also had to demonstrate other qualifications. Priests had to study religion and understand the Egyptian beliefs. They also had to belong to a family with other members who had served in the priesthood.

The Greek rulers chose Memphis as the center of their religion and the ancient capital of Egypt. It was located on the Nile River, in Middle Egypt. Temples there were dedicated to Ptah, the god of Memphis. The high priest of Ptah was a very powerful man in Egypt. A new pharaoh went south from Alexandria, up the Nile, to receive the blessing of the high priest at Memphis.

Another center of religion was Thebes. It was located far to the south of Memphis along the Nile. Thebes was the capital of Upper Egypt. This was the location of the Temple of Karnak. This large temple was

EGYPTIAN BURIAL PRACTICES

Egypt's burial practices were many centuries old. The Greeks did not generally participate in these practices. They usually preferred to be cremated after death. However, the Greek Ptolemies continued Egyptian burial practices. As foreign rulers, the Ptolemies realized that ancient religious traditions had to be maintained to keep the Egyptian people happy.

After their death, Egyptians had their bodies preserved as mummies. An opening was made in the side of a corpse. Through this opening, the internal organs were removed. The body was then embalmed by injecting natron, a salt solution. After embalming, the body was wrapped in linen cloth to keep it clean. A colorful mask of cloth and plaster might also be placed over the corpse's face. After a mummy was prepared, the family might keep it at home for a short period. Eventually, the mummy was carried by a group of undertakers to a cemetery for burying.

devoted to the Egyptian god Amon-Ra. He was the sun god, once the chief deity for all of Egypt. By the time of Ptolemy, however, Amon-Ra was only a local god at the city of Thebes.

Temples of the gods were also located in villages. Egyptian villagers worked on large estates that produced wheat and other crops to support the priests, who were among the most educated people in Egypt. Their temples were places where learning flourished and where they preserved Egypt's traditions.

The Ptolemies spent large sums of money to maintain the Egyptian temples. They respected the ancient Egyptian gods. But the Ptolemies also believed in worshiping new gods in Egypt. One was the Greek god Dionysus, the god of wine.

In Alexandria, a great celebration was staged in honor of Dionysus. The streets were lined with "mechanical statues . . . on huge floats," according to historian Robin Lane Fox, "wine ran freely over the streets from vast pitchers; sweet refreshments were given out to the spectators." There also "marched 2,000 oxen smothered in gold, 2,400 dogs, some giraffes, antelopes, Indian parrots, elephants . . . ostriches pulling carts."[5] In one parade, seventy-five thousand people in Alexandria drank, ate, and sang for two days.

Ptolemy I and II also made the worship of the god Serapis far more popular. Serapis is the combination of the Egyptian god Osiris and Zeus, the powerful chief god of the Greeks. Serapis was believed to have great powers to heal the sick and protect soldiers in battle. This god combined the cultures of Egypt and Greece. Great shrines and temples were dedicated to Serapis and other gods in Memphis and Alexandria. Gradually, the worship of Serapis became very popular throughout the Mediterranean world.

Another important goddess was Isis, the sister of Osiris. Egyptians believed that Isis made the land fertile to produce rich harvests. She also used her magic to protect people from evil. The Ptolemies built many

Egyptian Gods and Goddesses

There were dozens of gods and goddesses that the ancient Egyptians worshipped. Here are some of the most important.

Amon—King of the Gods to those who lived in and around Thebes.

Anubis—God of mummification.

Atum—God of the setting sun.

Geb—God of the earth.

Hathor—Goddess of love, music, and women.

Horus—God of the sun and the pharaohs.

Isis—Goddess of magic.

Nut—Goddess of the sky.

Osiris—God of the afterlife.

Ra—Creator god of the sun.

Seth—God of storms and chaos.

Shu—God of the air.

Tefnut—Goddess of moisture and rain.

Thoth—God of wisdom and the moon.

shrines in honor of Isis throughout Egypt. Isis also later became a very popular goddess throughout the Roman Empire.

Philadelphus also honored the memory of his father, Ptolemy Soter, who was considered a god. In 279 B.C., Philadelphus established a celebration called the Ptolemaieia. It was held in Alexandria every four years. Like the Olympic games established in Greece, the Ptolemaieia consisted of athletic contests. Poets and musicians also presented their works, and the winners were awarded prizes.

THE LIBRARY AND MUSEUM OF ALEXANDRIA

In addition to starting the Ptolemaieia, Ptolemy II (Philadelphus) also built the great library at Alexandria. The library was connected to the Museum. In Cleopatra's time, approximately seven hundred thousand manuscripts were housed at the huge library. Cleopatra probably used some of them in her education. The manuscripts were written on papyrus. This was a plant grown along the Nile River. Papyrus was harvested and cut into strips, which were pressed into a kind of paper. The papyrus scrolls were stored in ten giant halls that made up the library. "Texts became hot royal property," according to historian Robin Lane Fox. "When ships landed in Alexandria they were searched for books. Any found on board had to be surrendered for royal copying in scrolls stamped with the words 'from the ships.'"[6] The originals were kept in the library. A copy of the manuscript was given to the book's owner.

In addition to the library, Ptolemy II built the Lighthouse of Alexandria. As Cleopatra looked out on the island of Pharos, she could see the giant lighthouse. At four-hundred-feet tall, the lighthouse was considered one of the Seven Wonders of the Ancient World. Built of marble, the lighthouse was crowned by a magnificent statue of the Greek god Zeus. During the day, a giant mirror in the top of the lighthouse reflected the sun toward ships approaching the harbor. At night, a large fire was kept burning at the top of the lighthouse. This warned approaching ships that they were nearing the island. To avoid crashing on the rocks, they had to sail

Scholars at the Library of Alexandria cared for the many scrolls that were stored there.

The Great Lighthouse of Alexandria had a statue of Zeus at its top, and a bright fire burning within its tower at night.

around Pharos to enter the huge harbors at Alexandria. At least twelve hundred ships could anchor in the harbors at one time.

From her tutors, Cleopatra learned that Ptolemy II was not only a builder. He also expanded the Egyptian empire. He and his son, Ptolemy III, pushed the boundaries of Egypt into Syria and almost to India. Ptolemy III (246 B.C.–221 B.C.) was called Euergetes (The Benefactor) and later the Conqueror of the World.

 # THE DECLINE OF EGYPT

Over the next two centuries, the Egyptian empire began to decline. Several of the Ptolemies became rulers when they were only children. Others were far more interested in personal pleasure than in ruling an empire. Meanwhile, Egypt found itself facing a much stronger power—Rome.

During her studies with the tutors from the Museum, Cleopatra learned about the expansion of the Roman Empire. In the third century B.C., Rome had fought a long series of wars with Carthage, a trading city in North Africa. Carthage had a large fleet and colonies in Spain. Led by their general Hannibal, the Carthaginians had invaded Italy in 218 B.C. Roman armies were beaten time and again by Hannibal, but he was unable to conquer Rome. Eventually, a Roman army invaded North Africa and the Romans defeated the Carthaginians at the Battle of Zama in 201 B.C. Rome gained control of a large empire in Spain and North

Africa. During the next century, Roman armies also expanded their power into Asia Minor.

In 168 B.C., Egyptian pharaoh Ptolemy VI Philometer (180 B.C.–145 B.C.) had to ask for help from Rome. Egypt was being invaded by King Antiochus IV, who ruled in Syria. The Roman armies arrived just in the nick of time when Antiochus was only a few miles from Alexandria. According to the Greek historian Polybius, the Romans sent a representative, Gaius Popilius

KEEPING THE ROMANS HAPPY

The Ptolemies realized that it was important to make the Romans feel welcome in Alexandria. Roman ambassadors arrived in 140 B.C. The historian Diodorus said that "Ptolemy received them with great ceremony . . . preparing sumptuous banquets. He took them around the palace and showed them the royal quarters and the treasury." Afterward, the king showed the Roman delegation around Alexandria, and took them to the Pharos lighthouse. "Then they sailed up the river and noted carefully the richness of the land and the role of the Nile in this prosperity."

In 112 B.C., a prominent Roman official, Lucius Memmius, sailed to Egypt and was treated well by his Egyptian hosts. The Egyptian officials were instructed to make sure that "the guest-rooms are prepared and the landing places are ready, and present him there with gifts. . . . Make sure there is furniture in the guest-rooms. . . . In short, do your very best and take the greatest pains to see that this visitor is well-satisfied."[7]

Laenas, to Alexandria. He delivered an ultimatum to Antiochus, ordering him to leave. Antiochus wanted time to consider the order, but Laenas "drew a circle around Antiochus and told him that he must give a reply from within that circle. The king was outraged at the high-handedness of this act but, recovering his wits after a moment's pause, said that he would do everything that the Romans ordered."[8]

Once the threat from Antiochus was gone, a dispute broke out between Ptolemy VI and his brother for control of Egypt. Philometer, the pharaoh, was finally driven out and replaced by Ptolemy Physkon. Philometer went to Rome looking for help. The historian Diodorus described the sad state of the former king:

> Ptolemy [Philometer], king of Egypt, having been thrown from his kingdom by his own brother, arrived in Rome in the pitiful guise [clothes] of a simple citizen. . . . He lodged with a certain Demetrius who lived, because of the high city rents, in a little garret [apartment] at the top of a mean [poor] house.[9]

Rome stepped in again and split up the Egyptian kingdom between the two brothers.

Physkon received West Africa, while Philometer stayed in Egypt. He also ruled Cyprus, an island in the Mediterranean. Once Philometer died, Physkon came back to Alexandria and married Philometer's widow. After the wedding ceremony was over, Physkon murdered her son. This boy had been ruling the kingdom as Ptolemy VII. Then Physkon crowned himself Ptolemy VIII (146 B.C.–116 B.C.)

In 140 B.C., a Roman ambassador and his assistants who were sent to Egypt wrote a report to Rome. They were "astonished at the number of inhabitants of Egypt and the natural advantages of the countryside, [and] they perceived a mighty power could be sustained there if this kingdom ever found capable leaders."[10]

 # WEAKNESS IN EGYPT

During the half century before Cleopatra's birth, the situation inside Egypt worsened. Battles for the throne continued between rival members of the royal family. Among them was Cleopatra's great uncle, Ptolemy X, who was forced off the throne by Cleopatra's grandfather, Ptolemy IX. Ptolemy X fled to Rome where he raised a large amount of money to pay for a fleet to be built, but he died before he could attack Alexandria.

In 80 B.C., after the death of Ptolemy IX, the Romans supported a new king in Alexandria. He was Ptolemy XI, the son of Ptolemy X, who had been living in Rome. When he arrived in Alexandria, Berenike, the widow of Ptolemy IX, was in charge. The new pharaoh ordered her death, but Berenike was well-liked by the citizens of Alexandria. A short time after her murder, some Alexandrians rebelled against Ptolemy XI and killed him. Rome immediately found a new member of the royal family, who, backed by a Roman army, was crowned Ptolemy XII. This was Cleopatra's father, Ptolemy Auletes.

PTOLEMY AULETES

Auletes was forced to walk a very narrow line as king. He had to satisfy the demands of Rome, because the Romans had put him into power. However, he also had to listen to the people of Alexandria. The city was a mixture of various different people. Some were Greeks who worked as advisors and officials in the king's government. There were also Jewish merchants and artisans who lived in Alexandria. Finally, there were the many poor, who were mainly Egyptians. Their ancestors had lived in Egypt for thousands of years, when Egypt was run by powerful Egyptian pharaohs. The Egyptians resented the Greeks and also opposed the constant interference of Rome in the affairs of Egypt. Auletes had already seen the people of Alexandria overthrow one ruler.

In 64 B.C., a Roman army led by Gnaeus Pompeius invaded Syria. Known as Pompey the Great, he had become one of Rome's most successful commanders. Auletes feared that Pompey might not stop at Syria but continue on and invade Egypt. Auletes was afraid that Egypt would then become a permanent part of the Roman empire. To avoid this fate, Auletes immediately sent eight thousand Egyptian cavalry to help Pompey in his conquest of Palestine. Pompey left Egypt as an independent kingdom and supported Ptolemy Auletes.

Several years later, Auletes sent a large sum of money to another powerful Roman leader, Julius Caesar. In 59 B.C., Caesar was consul in Rome. Each year the Romans selected two consuls to lead the government.

Caesar began talking about making Egypt part of the Roman Empire. Auletes offered Rome eight thousand silver talents—about one-half of the pharaoh's annual income—to recognize him as king of Egypt.[11]

Auletes had to get the money to pay Rome by taxing the Egyptian people. The Egyptians were not happy about paying high taxes to Rome. They grew even angrier when the Romans decided to take control of the island of Cyprus. As a result of losing Cyprus, the people of Alexandria drove Auletes from the throne in 58 B.C.

Historian Michael Grant believes that the eleven-year-old Cleopatra may have fled Alexandria with her father, Auletes, and traveled to Rome.[12] There, Auletes hoped to persuade the Roman leaders to help him

MONEY IN THE ANCIENT WORLD

One of the primary units of money in the ancient world was a talent. This was an amount that equaled fifty-seven pounds of silver. There were also gold talents. A gold talent was far more valuable—about twelve times what a silver talent was worth. A talent was divided into six thousand drachmas (a Greek unit of money). Another name for the drachma was a Roman denarius. Both the drachma and the denarius were coins made of silver. The Egyptian drachma contained silver and bronze. Ptolemy Auletes reduced the value of the drachma by increasing the bronze content. The king controlled the Egyptian banks, so when the banks minted coins with more bronze, the king could keep more silver for himself.

recover his throne. Once again Auletes relied on bribes. He raised ten thousand talents, this time from a local banker named Gaius Rabirius Postumus. Auletes promised the ten thousand talents to the Roman governor in Syria, Aulus Gabinius, who had a strong army, in return for leading an invasion in Egypt. Auletes wanted the Romans to put him back on the throne, but many leading Egyptians did not want Auletes to return. When some Alexandrians arrived in Rome to oppose him, Auletes had them murdered.

Meanwhile, civil war had broken out in Egypt between two of Auletes' other daughters. Both claimed to be queen of the country. Eventually, one of the sisters died, and the other sister, Berenice IV claimed the throne. But her reign was very short. Gabinius invaded Egypt in 55 B.C. and put Auletes back on the throne in Alexandria, and no sooner had he returned to the city than he had Berenice executed. Murder and execution were quite common among the Ptolemies. These rulers believed that the only way to eliminate a rival was to kill him or her.

THE FORCES THAT SHAPED CLEOPATRA

By the time she was fourteen, Cleopatra had been shaped by a variety of experiences. Growing up in the shadow of the Museum and the Library of Alexandria, she had received an education fit for a ruler. Cleopatra considered herself Greek—the heir to Greek literature, science, and philosophy. However, she also recognized that neither Greece nor Egypt were among the world's great powers. Rome had become the center of the Mediterranean world. She had watched her father bargain with Rome to keep his throne. Therefore, Cleopatra probably realized that any Egyptian pharaoh in the future must do the same thing. The alternative was to lose the throne and put up with direct rule by the Romans. However, no Egyptian ruler could be seen as a Roman puppet—doing whatever Rome ordered. The Egyptian people might rise up and drive the pharaoh from the throne. They had driven out Auletes once. Cleopatra also recognized that she might need to resort to violence to defend her throne. Auletes had killed his own daughter, just as other Ptolemies had murdered members of their own families to remain in power.

In 51 B.C., Auletes was near death. The king made a will decreeing that he would be succeeded by Cleopatra and her eldest brother, who was only ten years old. Auletes died shortly afterward. Cleopatra, age eighteen, and her brother Ptolemy XIII became joint rulers. Cleopatra VII was now Queen of Egypt.

CLEOPATRA'S EGYPT

In 51 B.C., when Cleopatra became queen, she showed immediately that she intended to be a forceful, independent ruler. The new queen ignored her father's will, and decided to rule alone, without her brother, Ptolemy XIII, or his advisors. It was a daunting task for a young, inexperienced ruler. Egypt was a complex land, with a variety of cultures, religious beliefs, and economic interests. It was a nation threatened from the outside by powerful enemies. From the inside, Cleopatra faced constant turmoil.

One of Queen Cleopatra's first decisions was to travel up the Nile River. She sailed by boat to Thebes in Upper Egypt. This gave the new queen an opportunity to show herself to her subjects. Along the river, she passed many small villages where thousands of Egyptian peasants lived. In the first century B.C., Egypt was probably the most populous kingdom in the Mediterranean. According to one ancient historian, Diodorus Siculus, the population may have been as high as three million people. Villages were located about every two miles along the Nile River.[1]

Long before Cleopatra's day, Egyptians settled around the Nile River.

In summer, the Nile flooded over its banks. The villages were built on high mounds to avoid being swept away by the flood waters. Other villages were located along the tributaries of the Nile in the north. The waters from the Nile were collected in canals and behind dams to irrigate farmland. By October, the Nile waters began

QUEENS OF EGYPT

During the Ptolemaic period, Cleopatra VII was not the only powerful woman of her dynasty. Arsionoe II, wife of Ptolemy Philadelphus, had operated as a powerful advisor to her husband. In the past, pharaohs had sometimes died, leaving sons who were too young to rule. In these situations, the pharaoh's widow ruled Egypt. Cleopatra I had played this role after the death of her husband, Ptolemy V. Her son, Ptolemy VI, was still a child. Cleopatra VII's father, Ptolemy Auletes, had been driven from Egypt by the people of Alexandria. In his absence, one of Cleopatra's sisters was considered Egypt's ruler.

Women in Egypt had more freedom and power than those in Rome. Unlike Roman women, Egyptian women could inherit property from their fathers. They could also buy and sell property. A few women became philosophers, writers, and artists. In addition, Egyptian women were free to select their own husbands. In Rome, by contrast, women could not marry without the consent of their fathers. Romans were very critical of the freedom enjoyed by Egyptian women. They also criticized the power exercised by Egyptian queens.

to recede. Left behind was rich soil from the river. The farmers used this soil to grow their crops.

As Cleopatra traveled south, her boat passed Thebes. Then she stopped a few miles beyond the city at Hermonthis. This was a holy place where Egyptian priests maintained a temple dedicated to a god called Buchis. The god took the form of a large bull, but since the bull had died, the priests were replacing him with another bull. Cleopatra decided to attend the magnificent replacement ceremony. She wanted to show her support for the traditional gods of Egypt.

THE EGYPTIAN ANIMAL GODS

Buchis, the bull, was not the only animal that the Egyptians revered. A black bull with white spots, Apis of Memphis, was another important god to the Egyptians. In fact, when Apis died in 49 B.C., Cleopatra went to Memphis and attended the religious ceremony associated with his death. According to historian Guy Goudchaux, the queen made a contribution that included "412 silver coins . . . a measure of wine, a measure of milk and twelve loaves of bread for the clergy, and twenty-seven measures of oil . . . 50 measures of beans and 40 measures of another type of oil as well as payment for meat."[2]

In addition to bulls, the Egyptians considered the ibis to be sacred. These are large white birds with long legs. They are found along the Nile and lived in the major Egyptian cities, like Alexandria. The Nile was also home to large crocodiles. Among the Egyptian deities

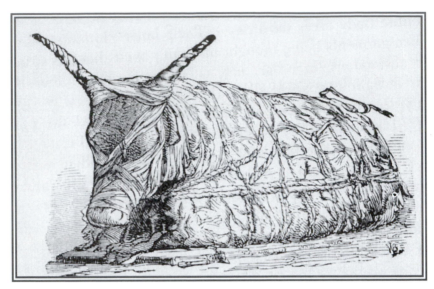

The god Apis of Memphis was represented by a real bull that Egyptians could visit. If the bull died, the sacred animal was mummified. Then, another bull was selected to represent Apis.

was the crocodile god, Sobek. On a tributary of the Nile, the Egyptians built a city called Krokodilopolis to honor Sobek. The crocodiles in the area were considered sacred. They were fed regularly by the local priests. In addition to crocodiles, the Egyptians also had a cat goddess, called Bastet. Indeed, the Egyptians believed that cats were sacred. During the reign of Cleopatra's father, a Roman living in Alexandria had mistakenly killed a cat. A vengeful Egyptian mob captured and immediately hanged the Roman.

When a sacred animal died, it was given an elaborate funeral. The Egyptians followed the same rituals in burying their people. The body was dried and mummified. Afterward, the corpse was wrapped in layers of white linen cloth. The mummy was then placed in a coffin. In Egypt, there was a centuries-old belief in life after death. Pharaohs were buried with food and clothing, as well as many of their servants, to sustain them in the afterlife. The Egyptian pharaohs were also buried inside giant tombs and pyramids. The Greeks, by contrast, did not have the same religious beliefs. They had little confidence that an afterlife, if it did exist, would be very pleasurable. Nor did the Ptolemies build

Egyptians considered cats very sacred. When a cat died, it was mummified (left and right). Egyptians also worshipped the cat goddess Bastet (represented in the center).

enormous tombs, like the pyramids, in which to bury their monarchs.

TEMPLES AND ORACLES

Cleopatra may not have shared the Egyptian beliefs, but she recognized the importance of supporting them. Temples, like those in Memphis, Thebes, and Hermonthis, were sacred to the Egyptians. The temples were not like modern churches. They were not places where Egyptians went for religious services. The temple was the home of a god. It was maintained by priests and priestesses, who were often the daughters of high-ranking government officials, according to historian Sarah Pomeroy.[3]

Most Egyptians prayed to their gods at home, where they kept small religious statues. They went to the temple grounds for religious festivals. During these festivals, the priests displayed large sculptures of the gods. People also visited the temples to consult an oracle. This was a holy person through which the god spoke and gave advice. Local villagers consulted the oracle if they faced an important decision, such as whether to get married. They submitted the problem to the oracle and then received an answer, generally written by the priests of the temple. In a period of uncertainty and turmoil, the oracle's answers helped give people a feeling of security.

The Egyptian gods and their temples had existed for thousands of years. The Ptolemaic rulers preserved these temples. They also supported the power of the Egyptian priests who ran them. Rulers like Cleopatra spent huge sums of money maintaining the temples and building new statues to the gods.

The temples had large landholdings that were worked by Egyptian peasants. On these lands the peasants grew wheat from which they produced flour that was made into bread. A variety of livestock, such as cows, chickens, sheep, and goats, was raised on the temple lands, too. The peasants also raised flax, a plant from which linen is made. The fiber from flax plants was woven into linen which was made into robes and other garments. In addition, the temple lands produced sesame and safflower plants, whose seeds were pressed to produce valuable oils. The oil was used as a fuel for sacred lamps and as an ingredient in cooking.

 # CLEOPATRA'S SUBJECTS

Most of Cleopatra's subjects were farmers. Some Egyptian peasants worked the land owned by the temples or by wealthy nobles. Because of the Nile and its yearly floods, Egypt was among the world's richest agricultural areas. The Egyptians not only produced enough wheat to feed themselves, but they also grew a huge surplus to export to other parts of the Mediterranean world. In addition to wheat, Egyptian farmers grew olive trees to make olive oil—a vital cooking ingredient. They also grew beans and peas, an essential part of the Egyptian diet. Large orchards produced dates and other fruits. Another important crop was barley, which the Egyptians used to make beer. They

This modern Egyptian demonstrates how his people farmed in ancient times.

also raised bees to make honey, as well as pigeons, their primary source of meat.

In addition to the Egyptian peasants, Greeks also farmed the land. Many were Greek soldiers, called cleruchs. They were given farms by the rulers in return for service in the army. Cavalry officers received between fourteen acres and fifty-four acres. Infantrymen received smaller plots. These soldiers were reservists: they could be called up by Cleopatra into the regular army if Egypt was threatened with invasion.

For the privilege of working the land, the Egyptian peasants had to pay rent to the nobles or the temples. Some also leased land that was owned by the Ptolemies.[4] According to historian Michel Chauveau, this amounted to about forty percent of their crop. In addition, peasants had to pay taxes to the king. As a result, the typical peasant was left with only about one third of his crop. Some peasants became so fed up with this situation that they went on strike. In 118 B.C., the king lowered the rent so the peasants would go back to work.[5]

Cleopatra's government imposed heavy taxes on her subjects. The taxes were paid in coins or in kind—that is, in agricultural products. The wheat and other food products were stockpiled in large storehouses. Cleopatra's government sold this surplus to other empires, such as Rome. Indeed, the Romans relied on Egyptian wheat to feed their people in Italy. Cleopatra used money collected as taxes to pay the royal army. In addition, the tax revenue was used to pay the learned men at the Museum and Library. Tax money also went into the cost of building marble palaces and paying the servants at the queen's royal court.

Not only farmers paid taxes. Merchants, artisans, and manufacturers also paid a heavy tax to the government. Some of these artisans made beautiful works of pottery and sculpture. In the area around Memphis, craftsmen made metal lamps and statues of bronze and gold. Other artisans made oil, while others produced papyrus. These were not independent producers who could sell their products in the marketplace. Cleopatra's government had a royal monopoly on the production of oil and papyrus. The government allowed only a small number of people to make these products which were then purchased by the government. The government sold them inside Egypt or exported them to other lands.

Government officials inspected all shops to make sure that no papyrus or oil was being sold illegally. In fact, the government ordered that the oil presses must be locked at night. This was to ensure that they could not be used to make extra products. In addition to oil and papyrus, the government also controlled the production of wool, linen, and many other goods. Only the temples were allowed to produce their own linen. This was used to make the priests' clothing.

While the monarchy grew rich, the peasants often suffered. As historian Michel Chauveau wrote, "these apparent riches concealed the dramatic misery of the countryside, where the most visible signs were the desertion of villages [by the peasants] and a lack of security even in the temples."[6]

 ## CLEOPATRA'S GOVERNMENT

To police the royal monopolies and run her government, Cleopatra maintained a large government with many levels of officials. The Ptolemies had inherited this government from the Egyptian pharaohs thousands of years earlier. Historians are not sure whether the central government arose to control the elaborate use of water from the Nile for irrigation projects or vice versa.[7]

When the Ptolemies took control of Egypt, they changed the government. Many officials they appointed were Greeks. However, Egyptians who learned Greek found jobs in the royal administration, too. The leading officials were known as the Kinsmen and the First Friends of the new kings. The most important government minister was the *dioketes*, the minister of finance. He was responsible for running of the districts in Egypt called *nomoi*. There were twenty nomoi in Lower Egypt and twenty-two in Upper Egypt.[8] Under Cleopatra and her predecessors, each nomoi was run by a Greek official called a *strategos*. He was in charge of a garrison of Greek troops that lived in each district. The strategos also had overall responsibility for making sure that taxes were collected. He ensured that irrigation systems operated properly and surplus food was stored in local warehouses. Frequently, the strategos passed on his authority to one of his sons. Therefore, the position might stay in the same family for generations.

The strategos had a huge responsibility, and he relied on other officials to help him. Perhaps the most important of these was the royal scribe, who was usually an Egyptian who could speak with the local farmers.[9] The scribe usually went out into the fields to look over the crops. He inspected the irrigation systems, and insured that the royal interests were protected.

Greeks and Egyptians worked together in the royal administration. But both groups generally led separate lives in Cleopatra's Egypt. When Greeks went to live in a village, they established a local club to build a gymnasium where they maintained Greek culture. They also participated in their own athletic games apart from the Egyptians. Greeks rarely learned to read the Egyptian language. Cleopatra was the exception. Instead, Greeks read their own poetry, such as Homer's *Iliad*, the story of the Trojan War, and the *Odyssey*, the epic story of the Greek hero Odysseus. They performed the plays of Greek writers, such as Sophocles and Aeschylus. And they read the works of Greek philosophers, such as Aristotle and Plato. As historian Michel Chauveau has written, Egyptian and Greek culture "coexisted like two completely partitioned worlds . . . [that] could not really be blended together."[10]

CLEOPATRA'S EARLY REIGN

Cleopatra began her reign by acting as sole ruler of Egypt, but problems quickly arose. First of all, the annual flood of the Nile was lower than usual. As one Roman historian wrote, "Seven metres [almost 23 feet] is an average rise. Less does not irrigate all the available land. . . . In a rise of five and a half metres [about 18 feet] one sees the specter of famine, and even in six meters

The flooding of the Nile was often celebrated with music. It signified the beginning of a new growing season. The man on the left burns incense to celebrate.

48

[over 9 feet] hunger is felt."[11] As a result, the harvest was poor. Indeed, Alexandria was threatened with food shortages that year.[12]

In addition, Cleopatra had to maintain an uneasy relationship with the Roman Empire. The Romans had advanced as far south as Syria, just to the east of Egypt. However, the Roman army feared an invasion from the Parthians—a powerful empire located to the east, around the Caspian Sea. In order to defend the area,

THE FADING BRILLIANCE OF ALEXANDRIA

During the last two centuries of Ptolemaic rule, the reputation of Alexandria as a center of learning declined. During the second century B.C., Ptolemy VIII ordered scholars to leave Alexandria. Historians are uncertain why he made this decision. The Egyptian civil wars that followed made Alexandria an unsafe place for scholars. Eventually some of the scholars returned.

One scholar does stand out during the reign of Cleopatra. Didymos came from a poor, uneducated family. Somehow he received an education and obtained a position at the Museum in Alexandria. Didymos was an expert on the works of Homer. He wrote many scholarly books on the poetry in the *Iliad* and the *Odyssey*. He also wrote works on the speeches of Demosthenes, a Greek orator who lived in the fourth century B.C. Indeed, Didymos composed almost four thousand books that were stored at the library in Alexandria.

the Roman governor of Syria, Bibulus, asked for reinforcements.

Gabinius had brought an army of Roman soldiers to Egypt several years earlier to help Ptolemy Auletes take back his throne. In 50 B.C., Bibulus sent his two sons to Egypt to work with Cleopatra and transfer these soldiers to Syria. However, the soldiers refused to go and murdered the sons of Bibulus.

Cleopatra acted swiftly. She arrested the murderers and sent them to Bibulus. However, the queen was resented by many of the Egyptian people for giving in to Rome. In addition, the Roman soldiers in Egypt believed that she should not have turned over the murderers to Bibulus. These soldiers now threatened to push Cleopatra out of Alexandria.

As a result, Cleopatra's position on the throne of Egypt was weakened considerably. The queen also faced a threat from her brother, Ptolemy XIII. About this same time, Ptolemy XIII seems to have begun ruling jointly with her. Ptolemy's advisors used the resentment felt by many of the Egyptian people to force Cleopatra to give up some of her power. Historian Michael Grant believes that powerful officials in Alexandria opposed her. In addition, since Ptolemy XIII was still too young to rule on his own, his power was being exercised by a strong group of aristocrats called a Regency Council. Cleopatra now faced a combination of forces that threatened to drive her out of Alexandria, just like her father, Ptolemy Auletes.[13]

CLEOPATRA AND ROME

During the next few years, Cleopatra fought to keep her power in Egypt. Meanwhile, she was caught up in a titanic struggle within the Roman Empire. Two men, Julius Caesar and Pompey the Great, were contending for control of the empire. Cleopatra supported first one, then the other, as she also tried to hold onto her own kingdom.

 ## POMPEY

For more than two decades—approximately 75 B.C. to 50 B.C.—Caesar and Pompey were the two most prominent men in Rome. Born in 106 B.C., Gnaeus Pompeius, known as Pompey the Great, was the son of Gnaeus Pompeius Strabo, a successful general and a leading Roman politician. Pompey spent his boyhood traveling with his father on military campaigns and learning about Roman politics. When Strabo died in 83 B.C., Pompey inherited a large sum of money from his father. He also received the support of Strabo's troops. Pompey used these troops to put down revolts in Sicily and Africa. In return for these victories, Pompey asked the Roman Senate for a triumph. This was a celebration in Rome to proclaim his victories. At first they said no, but Pompey threatened to bring his troops into Rome. As a result, the Senate finally agreed.

In 73 B.C., Pompey distinguished himself in the Roman province of Spain by putting down a revolt. No sooner had this problem been solved than Rome faced a slave rebellion. Slaves captured by the Romans during their wars were brought to Rome. They worked in the fields and as household servants. Some of the slaves also became gladiators. These men fought to the death in huge spectacles to entertain Roman audiences. One of these gladiators, named Spartacus, led a revolt that lasted two years. Finally, Spartacus was defeated in 71 B.C. by Pompey and Marcus Licinius Crassus, a wealthy merchant.

Following their victory, Pompey and Crassus were elected consuls. Each year, two consuls were elected to run the government with the help of the Senate and various assemblies. After serving as consul, Pompey was given command of Roman fleets in the Mediterranean in 67 B.C. His job was to attack and destroy the pirates who had disrupted Roman shipping for many years.

The ancient historian Plutarch wrote that these pirates had not only been capturing

> merchants and ships upon the seas, but also [laying] waste the islands and seaport towns. . . . They had [many] arsenals, or piratic harbors, as likewise watch-towers and beacons, all along the sea-coast; and fleets were here

received that were well manned with the finest mariners, and well served with the expertest pilots, and composed of swift-sailing and light-built vessels adapted for their special purpose. . . . Their ships had gilded masts at their stems; the sails woven of purple, and the oars plated with silver. . . ." In addition to attacking ships, pirates also seized wealthy Roman citizens. Two politicians were captured "in their purpled-edged robes, and carried . . . off together. . . . The daughter also of Antonius, a man that had had the honor of a triumph, taking a journey to the country, was seized, and redeemed upon payment of a large ransom.[1]

Pompey took control of the Roman navy. Then, he divided up his ships into thirteen squadrons. Each squadron was given control of a different part of the Mediterranean. These squadrons captured many pirate ships. The Romans also seized control of the harbors used by pirates, and executed their leaders. By the end of 67 B.C., Pompey eliminated most of the pirate threat from the Mediterranean.

Fresh from this victory, Pompey headed east, where he defeated King Mithridates VI, the King of Pontus, a powerful kingdom around the Black Sea. The armies of Pontus often threatened to invade the Roman Empire. Pompey took the king's huge treasure, worth many thousands of talents. About twenty thousand talents went to the Roman treasury. But Pompey also kept some of the money for himself, making him an extremely rich man. From there, Pompey went southwest, taking control of Syria and Jerusalem in 63 B.C. At about this time, he gave his support to Ptolemy Auletes to keep the Egyptian kingdom independent.

 JULIUS CAESAR

While Pompey was winning victories in the east, Julius Caesar had been pursuing his own political career. Born in 100 B.C., Caesar was a member of an aristocratic family, the Julii. His uncle was Caius Marius, a very successful Roman general who had been elected consul seven times. As a boy, Caesar was tutored at home. He learned to speak Greek and wrote poetry. According to the historian Suetonius, at age sixteen, Caesar was a "tall, fair and well-built" young man.[2] In his early twenties, Caesar served with the Roman legions on the Greek island of Lesbos. The legions were putting down a rebellion on the island, part of the Roman Empire. Caesar received a special medal for bravery in battle.

Following his army service, Caesar returned to Rome, entered the legal profession and began defending clients. He rapidly earned a reputation "as one of the greatest orators [speakers] of his time," according to historian Ernle Bradford.[3] His popularity increased throughout the city. As Plutarch wrote:

> . . . his eloquence soon obtained him great credit and favor, and he won no less upon the affections of the people by the affability [friendliness] of his manners . . . in which he showed a tact and consideration beyond what could have been expected at his age; and the open house he kept, the entertainments he gave, and the

general splendor of his manner of life contributed little
by little to create and increase his political influence.[4]

In 75 B.C., however, Caesar became a victim of the
Mediterranean pirates. They held him for a ransom of
twenty talents. Caesar said that he was worth more than
this amount. Therefore the pirates asked for fifty talents.
After they received the ransom, the pirates released him.
However, Caesar gathered a small force, pursued the
pirates, and killed them.[5]

Caesar was a champion of the common people. He
spent money to provide them with public feasts and
outdoor theater. Caesar also supported their demands
for more power. These demands were opposed by the
wealthy Roman aristocrats who controlled the Senate.
By 67 B.C., Caesar himself had become a senator. That
same year, he also took up a military post in Spain. The
historian Suetonius wrote that when Caesar was there he
"saw a statue of Alexander the Great . . . and was heard
to give a great sigh. It would seem that he was despon-
dent because, at an age when Alexander had already
conquered the whole world, he himself had done nothing
of any importance."[6]

Caesar returned to Rome, where he supported
Pompey. He believed that Pompey was the best man to
eliminate the pirates in the Mediterranean and to defeat
Mithridates. Like Pompey, Caesar wanted to be consul.
In 63 B.C., he took an important step in that direction.
Caesar was elected Pontifex Maximus, the chief priest of
Rome. This was a powerful political position.

Meanwhile, Caesar had become a friend not only of Pompey but also of the wealthy Crassus. With their support, Caesar ran a successful campaign for consul in 59 B.C. Caesar then brought Pompey and Crassus together in a three-way alliance. This political alliance was called the First Triumvirate. Later that year, Pompey married Caesar's daughter, Julia. This marriage cemented the alliance between Caesar and Pompey. Caesar also pushed through legislation in the Senate rewarding Pompey's soldiers who had defeated Mithridates. They were given land for their own farms.

As his consulship ended, Caesar was appointed to command the Roman armies in the province of Gaul (present-day France). In this position (58 B.C.–50 B.C.) he defeated the local tribes, including the Helvetii, the Belgae, and the Arverni. Caesar also captured a leading general, Vercingetorix. Caesar's campaigns were noted for rapid marches over tough terrain, the bravery of his soldiers who withstood many hardships, and his courageous leadership. These factors enabled him to beat the enemy time and again. Caesar's book, *The Gallic Wars,* described the campaigns and made him famous throughout Italy. Caesar also invaded the island of Britain in 55 B.C.–54 B.C. It was the first time a Roman army had set foot on the island. However, he was unable to defeat the local tribes and finally withdrew to Gaul.

CIVIL WAR SPREADS TO EGYPT

Meanwhile, Crassus had taken command of the Roman armies in the east. He had been given the responsibility

Roman Legions

The backbone of the army that Caesar commanded in Gaul was the Roman legion. A legion, at full strength, consisted of six thousand soldiers. Every soldier carried his own sword and spear. The sword was double-sided, with a sharp edge on each side. For protection, soldiers wore metal helmets. They also carried shields made of leather and wood. In addition, each soldier carried his own food and entrenching tools.  These tools were used to build a fortified camp with deep trenches around it.

The legions were led by career officers, known as centurions. These were battle-hardened veterans who rarely retired or were discharged. Each centurion commanded a group of eighty men, called a century. Six of these centuries were formed into a cohort. There were ten cohorts in a legion. The senior officers of a legion included a legate, a tribune, and a prefect.

In addition to infantry, or foot soldiers, a well-trained cavalry unit accompanied the Roman legions. (Cavalry were soldiers on horses.) Caesar's army also carried siege equipment, including battering rams to knock down the walls of enemy cities. There were catapults as well, large contraptions that hurled huge rocks at the enemy.

of defeating an invasion by Parthia. This was a powerful kingdom located near the Caspian Sea. However, Crassus and his army were destroyed in 53 B.C. This left Pompey and Caesar as the most powerful men in Rome. By this time, both men had become jealous of each other's success. Caesar's daughter Julia, married to Pompey, had died in 54 B.C. This removed an important bond between the two men. What is more, the Roman Senate feared that Caesar wanted to make himself a military dictator. Pompey had the support of the Senate, which preferred him to Caesar.

Late in 50 B.C., the Senate ordered Caesar to leave his army and return to Italy, an order Caesar disobeyed. He feared what might happen to him without the protection of his army. On January 10, 49 B.C., Caesar left Gaul. Along with one of his legions, Caesar crossed the Rubicon River, dividing Gaul and Italy. According to Roman law, a general was not permitted to lead an army out of the provinces into Italy. But Caesar supposedly said, "The die is cast,"[7] meaning his fate was sealed. He believed that without an army, his future was in jeopardy at the hands of the Senate. Therefore, he decided to march on Rome in defiance of the law. Many people in Italy supported him. He quickly swept southward with very little opposition and entered Rome.

Meanwhile, Pompey and most of the Senate had left Italy. Pompey commanded a large fleet and took his soldiers to northern Greece. Pompey also controlled another army in the province of Spain. As historian John Leach wrote, "Once in Greece it was Pompey's plan to maintain a naval blockade on Italy, and trap Caesar between two great armies. . . ."[8]

But nothing went according to plan. Caesar rushed to Spain, where he defeated armies allied to Pompey. Caesar then went back to Rome, where he began to gather his troops to attack Pompey in Greece.

In preparation for the coming battle, Pompey tried to build a large army. He planned to overwhelm Caesar's forces. As the man who had conquered much of the eastern Mediterranean, Pompey had achieved great prestige in that part of the world. The soldiers stationed in the eastern provinces supported him. Pompey had also developed a strong relationship with Egypt. He had supported Cleopatra's father, Auletes, and championed the independence of Egypt. Pompey sent his son to Alexandria with a request for support in his battle against Caesar. Cleopatra remembered that Pompey and her father had been friends. She also believed that Pompey's army was stronger than Caesar's. Therefore, Cleopatra decided that Egypt's best interests lay with backing Pompey. She decided to send him troops and supplies.

When the people of Alexandria learned about Cleopatra's decision, they were furious. In the past they had driven out Auletes for cooperating with Rome. They also resented Cleopatra's willingness to hand over the murderers of Bibulus's sons. Meanwhile, Cleopatra's young brother, Ptolemy XIII, and his advisors plotted against her. These men wanted to see Ptolemy XIII as Egypt's sole ruler. The boy's advisors believed that they could control him. By mid-year, 49 B.C., these forces combined to drive Cleopatra off the throne of Egypt. Ptolemy XIII now ruled without her, along with his council of advisors. They included his chief minister, Ponthinus, who was strongly committed to safeguarding Egypt's independence from Rome.

Cleopatra fled south along the Nile to Thebes. Here the queen still had strong support among the Egyptian people. She succeeded in raising a small army. Cleopatra then led the army to a position east of Alexandria. The army camped along the Nile outside the town of Pelusium. Here she prepared to face a more powerful army controlled by Ptolemy XIII and waited for the right moment to do battle for her throne.

Meanwhile, the civil war between Pompey and Caesar was reaching a climax. Pompey had raised a large army, of about forty thousand men. In addition, some of the local rulers, like Cleopatra, had also sent him troops. The historian Plutarch wrote that

> the infantry was a mixture of inexperienced soldiers drawn from different quarters, and these he [Pompey] exercised and trained . . . himself noways slothful, but performing all his exercises as if he had been in the flower of his youth, conduct which raised the spirits of his soldiers extremely. For it was no small encourage-ment for them to see Pompey the Great, sixty years of age wanting two, at one time handling his arms among the foot [infantry], then again mounted among the horse [cavalry], drawing out his sword with ease in full career, and sheathing it up as easily; and in darting [throwing] the javelin [long spear], showing not only skill and dexterity in hitting the mark, but also strength

and activity in throwing it so far that few of the young
men went beyond him.[9]

BATTLE OF PHARSALUS

While Pompey trained his army, Caesar's forces
advanced toward him. The two armies met at Pharsalus,
in Greece, on August 9, 48 B.C. Pompey placed his
cavalry on the flank, giving them a simple task when the
battle started. "I have persuaded our cavalry," he said,
"as soon as they get to close quarters, to attack Caesar's
right wing from its unprotected flank, surround his line
from the rear and throw it into confusion and rout it
before we have time to cast a single javelin at the
enemy." But Caesar proved more than a match for his
opponent. As historian John Leach wrote,

> When his cavalry did charge . . . the Caesarian cavalry
> steadily gave way. As the Pompeians began to wheel to
> the right to come around behind . . . they were suddenly
> met by a charge from . . . infantry which Caesar had
> withdrawn from his rear and kept hidden behind his
> cavalry. . . . Using their javelins as stabbing spears, and
> apparently aiming at the faces of the Pompeians, they
> created panic in the massed ranks of horsemen and
> routed them completely.[10]

Caesar's forces kept advancing behind Pompey's lines,
causing havoc. Pompey's forces began fleeing the field,
giving Caesar a decisive victory.

Pompey quickly gathered together a few of his
supporters and headed south. He was hoping to find
refuge in Egypt. On September 28, Pompey approached

the shoreline of Egypt. Here Ptolemy XIII's army was resting in camp. A small boat was sent out by the Egyptian ruler to meet Pompey. As Pompey stepped into the boat, he recognized one of the ambassadors from Ptolemy. This was a man named Lucius Septimius. The other two men in the boat were Achillas, Ptolemy's general, and a soldier named Salvius. Pompey said goodbye to his wife, who had accompanied him after the battle of Pharsalus. Then he was rowed toward shore.

Along the way, Pompey read over a short speech. He planned to deliver it to Ptolemy, thanking him for his support. But before the boat reached the shore, Pompey was suddenly stabbed to death by Septimius. Ptolemy and his advisors had decided that it was not safe to provide support for the no-longer powerful Pompey. By harboring him in Egypt, Ptolemy risked angering Caesar, who might march south and occupy the country. As one of Ptolemy's advisors told him, "dead men don't bite."[11] This meant that once Pompey the Great was dead, he could no longer create any threat to Ptolemy XIII and his advisors.

Ptolemy XIII now awaited the arrival of Caesar. His advance into Egypt would not only affect Ptolemy's rule. It would also transform the life of his sister Cleopatra.

CLEOPATRA, PTOLEMY, AND CAESAR

Shortly after the murder of Pompey, Caesar advanced into Egypt. The Romans played an important role in the war between Ptolemy and Cleopatra. Caesar and Cleopatra eventually developed a close relationship that enabled her to regain power.

 ## THE ADVANCE OF CAESAR

Early in October, 48 B.C., Caesar and part of his army sailed along the Mediterranean into Alexandria. He was met by one of Ptolemy's ambassadors, Theodotus. The ambassador brought Caesar a present, wrapped in cloth. When Caesar unwrapped the gift, he was horrified to see Pompey's head and his ring. He wept.[1] If the Egyptians had thought to please Caesar, they were mistaken. Pompey and Caesar had been enemies, but Caesar still regarded Pompey as a noble warrior. In the past, Caesar had supported him and Caesar's daughter had even been married to Pompey. The two men had worked together in the First Triumvirate, and together they had battled the enemies of Rome.

Caesar now found himself facing one of those enemies—the people of Alexandria. They resented the presence of another Roman in Egypt. The Egyptian people were also suffering from a famine due to an extremely bad harvest. In addition, Caesar had come to Alexandria partly to collect a huge debt still owed to Rome by Auletes. The pharaoh had borrowed the money to raise a huge army and regain his throne. But Auletes had died without ever paying it back. Caesar hoped to be paid this money. He wanted to reward his soldiers for defeating Pompey. But the people of Alexandria had no interest in paying off Caesar's soldiers. When they saw Caesar and his legions entering Alexandria, they were furious. The crowds expressed their fury by rioting in the city streets, killing some of Caesar's men.

Caesar headed for the protection of the Egyptian royal palace. He also sent out messages to some of his troops in Greece to hurry south, as reinforcements. Inside the palace, Caesar met with Ptolemy XIII and his advisor, Ponthinus. Caesar planned to enforce the will of the king's father, Auletes, as Rome had been asked to do. Auletes had wanted Ptolemy to share the throne with his sister Cleopatra.

However, according to historian Plutarch, Ponthinus was opposed to Caesar's meddling in the affairs of Egypt and showed his dislike of Caesar:

both by his words and actions. For when Caesar's soldiers had musty and unwholesome corn measured out to them, Ponthinus told them they must be content with it, since they were fed at another's cost. He ordered that his table should be served with wooden and earthen dishes, and said Caesar had carried off all the gold and silver plate[s] under pretence of arrears [paying off] of debt.[2]

THE ALEXANDRIA CAESAR SAW

When Caesar entered Alexandria, he saw one of the world's great cities. The geographer Strabo lived there at about the same time as Caesar's visit. Strabo described Alexandria this way:

. . . the city contains most beautiful public precincts and also the royal palaces, which constitute one-fourth or even one-third of the whole circuit of the city; for just as each of the kings, from love of splendor, was wont to add some adornment to the public monuments, so also he would invest himself at his own expense with a residence, in addition to those already built, so that now, to quote the words of the poet, "there is building upon building." All, however, are connected with one another and the harbor. . . . The Museum is also a part of the royal palaces; it has a public walk, [a theater] with seats, and a large house, in which is the common mess-hall of the men of learning who share the Museum. . . . The Soma also, as it is called, is a part of the royal palaces. This was the enclosure which contained the burial-places of the kings and that of Alexander. . . .[3]

Eventually, Caesar and his bodyguards decided to leave the palace to tour Alexandria. Caesar spoke in Greek with the people of the city, trying to improve relations with them. Caesar also visited the Museum and the Library. He was a learned man and understood many of the ideas discussed by the Greek scientists and philosophers there, and he asked them about their observations.[4]

 ## CLEOPATRA AND HER BROTHER

After his return to the palace, Caesar summoned Cleopatra to meet with him. She managed to slip through Ptolemy's army and enter the palace secretly. Cleopatra impressed Caesar with her intelligence, her wit, and her female charms. Caesar decided that Cleopatra and her brother Ptolemy should continue to rule together. Ptolemy was very upset with this decision. He realized that Caesar and Cleopatra had become engaged in a romantic relationship. Ptolemy stormed out of the palace, threw his crown on the ground, and tried to stir up the people of Alexandria against the Romans.[5] However, Caesar's men went after Ptolemy and brought him back inside the palace. In order to appease the Egyptians, Caesar gave back the island of Cyprus to Ptolemy. He put Arsinoe, another sister of the king, and his brother Ptolemy XIV in charge of ruling the island. They were living in the palace at Alexandria at the time.

However, Ptolemy and his advisor Ponthinus were not satisfied. They sent messages to General Achillas, who was in charge of the Egyptian army. Achillas led his troops into Alexandria. Then the army began to lay siege to Caesar's forces inside the palace. In *The Alexandrian Wars*, one of Caesar's officers wrote about the battle that took place. He said that Achillas' soldiers "shut up all the avenues and passes by a triple wall built of square stones, and carried to the height of forty feet. They defended the lower parts of the town by very high towers of ten stories." They also used "moving towers" drawn by horses to approach the palace so archers could shoot into it. Achillas cut off the water supply to the palace. Instead he filled the canals with salt water from the Mediterranean. This caused "a terror . . . among

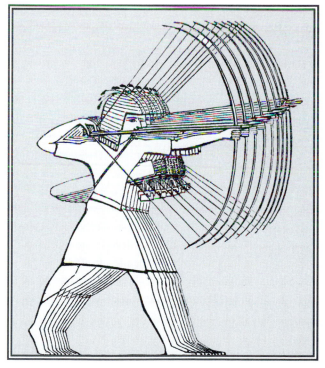

Achillas's archers rained down arrows on Caesar's soldiers from atop high towers.

[Caesar's] troops." However, Caesar ordered his soldiers to begin digging wells along the shore. There they found new sources of fresh water.[6]

Achillas also controlled a large fleet, which was threatening to sink the Roman ships Caesar had brought with him. However, Caesar led a surprise attack on the enemy ships and set them on fire. Unfortunately, the fire spread and destroyed some of the houses in the city. Although the Library at Alexandria seemed threatened by the flames, it was not harmed.

While the battle raged outside the palace, inside Ponthinus was planning to poison Caesar. The plot, however, was discovered by Caesar's barber, who overheard the conspirators. Ponthinus was immediately arrested and executed. Caesar also decided to let Arsinoe leave the palace along with her chief advisor, Ganymede. Caesar knew that Arsinoe and Achillas did not like each other. Indeed, Ganymede and Arsinoe began to plot against Achillas, after arriving at his camp. They eventually murdered Achillas.

Ganymede and Arsinoe, using Achillas' army, continued to press the attack on Caesar. They besieged the palace, with Caesar and Cleopatra inside. The Egyptians also tried to control the harbor with a large fleet. With his own ships, Caesar led a surprise attack on the Egyptian's warships. The Romans set most of them on fire. Meanwhile, Caesar began to improve his position at Alexandria with a successful assault on Pharos. This piece of land, with its famous lighthouse, controlled the entrance to the harbor at Alexandria. Caesar also tried to capture the long isthmus leading out

ANCIENT WARSHIPS

Warships during the first century B.C. were long galleys. Egyptian coins in this period show the long galleys with their banks of many oars. 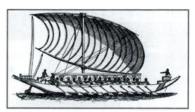 Many of the galleys were biremes. That is, they had two rows of oars. These were rowed by fifty to eighty men, usually slaves. In addition to the biremes, some ancient warships were triremes. That is, they had three rows of oars. In front of each galley was a high prow—or bow of the ship. Each galley also had one or two sails. Cleopatra's ships had purple sails. The sails enabled the ships to take advantage of the wind. With no winds, however, the galleys had to rely on the oarsmen.

In addition to the rowers, the ships also contained marines. These marines fired arrows, hurled javelins, or fought in hand-to-hand combat. As a galley approached an enemy warship, the two ships were lashed together with hooks and ropes. Then the marines boarded the enemy ship and tried to capture it.

Egyptian galleys also carried catapults. These machines hurled huge stones at enemy ships. Some of the galleys also had long battering rams, coated with bronze, attached to the front just below the water. The rams were used to sink enemy ships.

to the lighthouse. However, he was attacked by enemy troops and almost lost his life. As Caesar stepped into a small boat to leave the isthmus, many other Roman soldiers joined him. Caesar realized that the boat might sink. Therefore, in full armor, he jumped into the water. Then he swam several hundred yards to one of his ships in the harbor. This required great strength for any man. Since Caesar was over fifty, a swim in full armor showed that he was in remarkable physical shape.

Meanwhile, King Ptolemy had been pleading with Caesar to let him leave the palace. According to Cassius Dio, Caesar finally agreed because "he saw no source of strength in the lad," and hoped that the Egyptians might call off the war if they had Ptolemy back among them.[7] But the king immediately took over command of his army.

By this time, however, Caesar had received word that Roman reinforcements had arrived outside Alexandria. Caesar took his troops out of the city by ship and linked up with his reinforcements near Memphis on the Nile River. On March 27, 47 B.C., Caesar defeated the enemy army in a brutal two-day battle. As the Egyptians fled from the battlefield, Ptolemy drowned in the Nile River.

 ## CAESAR AND CLEOPATRA

Cleopatra resumed her position as the primary ruler of Egypt. Caesar insisted that she rule together with her younger brother, Ptolemy XIV, who was only about ten. However, Cleopatra paid no attention to her brother.

Instead Caesar and Cleopatra began a long trip south along the Nile River. They traveled on the queen's giant barge. It may have been similar to the giant luxury boat built by Ptolemy IV. This boat was three hundred feet in length, with luxurious cabins, fine food, and magnificent furniture. The barge was accompanied by a Roman army. Many of the Egyptians were still hostile to Caesar, and might have attacked the barge. Some of the Egyptians also resented Cleopatra for cooperating with Caesar.

After the tour of Egypt had ended, Caesar left the country. Behind him he left three legions under the command of Rufio. These legions were designed to safeguard Cleopatra's throne and to preserve Roman control of the country. He also left Cleopatra with a new son, whom she called Caesarion. Julius Caesar was probably Caesarion's father. The son was not welcomed by the people of Alexandria. But Cleopatra traveled south to the ancient religious center of Thebes, where she had more support. Here Caesarion was honored as a god by the priests of Amon-Ra.

While Cleopatra remained in Egypt, Caesar battled the remainder of Pompey's supporters in Africa. They were defeated in 46 B.C. Then Caesar returned to Rome. The Romans gave Caesar a spectacular triumph for his many victories. Forced to march in the parade was Arsinoe, the sister of Cleopatra. She had been made a prisoner after the defeat of Ptolemy. Arsinoe was bound in chains as she walked in the parade.

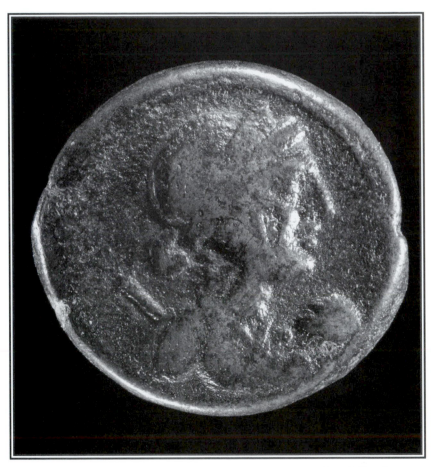

Cleopatra's image was engraved on this bronze coin while she was queen. It depicts her as Aphrodite, the goddess of love, and shows her holding her son Caesarion.

CLEOPATRA IN ROME

Late in 46 B.C., Cleopatra arrived in Rome. She brought her son, Caesarion, and her brother, Ptolemy XIV. Cleopatra and Caesarion lived in one of Caesar's homes outside of Rome. Although he had welcomed her in Rome, Caesar had no intention of marrying Cleopatra. Indeed, Caesar was already married. But Cleopatra hoped that by being in Rome, the Senate would renew the treaty that Rome had signed with her father to safeguard the independence of Egypt. As a friend of Caesar's, Cleopatra became a welcome celebrity in Rome and the treaty was quickly renewed.

At Caesar's home Cleopatra entertained many of the leading poets and political leaders of Rome. Along with her came several of the leading scientists of Alexandria, including the astronomer Sosigenes. Together with Sosigenes, Caesar developed a new calendar for Rome, which was similar to the calendar of the Egyptians. The old Roman calendar had only 355 days, because it was based on the phases of the moon. The new calendar, which is used today, was based on the sun. Each year has 365 days plus one extra day every four years. A year that has an extra day is called a leap year.

From his experience in Alexandria, Caesar had also learned about the importance of supplying water to a large city. Therefore, he began projects to develop new aqueducts for the people of Rome. Caesar also started planning large libraries in the city, much like the Library of Alexandria.

THE DEATH OF CAESAR

Caesar was the leader of the Roman Republic but he was also a dictator. He had become rich from the treasures of the wealthy kings whom he had conquered. Caesar had the loyalty of the powerful Roman army. In the Senate, he sat on a golden throne. In 44 B.C., his close friend, Mark Antony, presented Caesar with a crown in the Senate. Although he refused the crown, Caesar clearly acted like a king. In fact, many Romans feared that he wanted to be king.

In past centuries, Romans had fought to prevent kings from controlling the government. They believed in distributing power among the Senate, the consuls, and assemblies elected by the Roman people. Rumors also began to circulate in Rome that Caesar planned to make his new capital in Alexandria. Some Romans distrusted Cleopatra. She represented the east—a Greek instead of a Roman. Many Romans resented the relationship between Cleopatra and Caesar. They were also angry when Caesar dedicated a statue of Cleopatra at a new temple in the center of Rome. As historian Michel Chauveau wrote:

> Dedicating a statue in a temple to a sovereign or to a distinguished individual was a widespread practice in the . . . East, where this form of homage was held in high esteem. We may imagine that in Rome, rendering such an honor to a foreign queen was not to the taste of all, but it is clear that this was but one small object of discontent in . . . making the Roman state seem more and more like an Eastern monarchy.[8]

A group of the leading politicians, including many senators, believed that Caesar had already been given too much power. They were fearful that Caesar would eliminate all the old republican institutions. Led by Marcus Brutus and Lucius Cassius, they planned to assassinate Caesar. On March 15, 44 B.C., Caesar came to the Senate for a special meeting. As he walked into

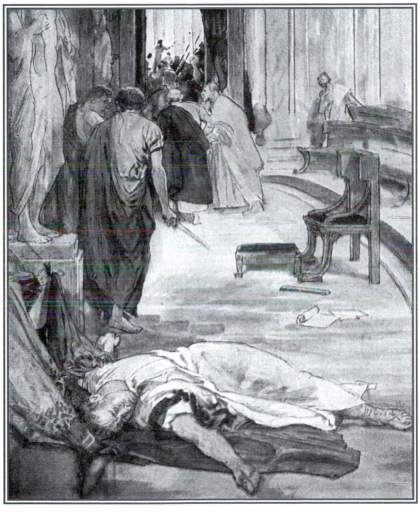

Caesar was stabbed several times by his attackers.

CLEOPATRA'S REACTION TO CAESAR'S DEATH

The ancient historians, such as Plutarch, tell us little about Cleopatra's response to the assassination of Caesar. Suddenly, the queen's powerful defender was dead. There was no leader in Rome to give her any protection. Nevertheless, Cleopatra remained in Rome, at least for a short period. On April 5, several weeks after the assassination, Cicero wrote, "I see nothing to object to in the Queen's flight."[9] Cicero did not like Cleopatra and would have been happy to see her return to Egypt.

the Senate chamber, he was surrounded by the assassins. They began stabbing him repeatedly with their daggers until he was dead.

With the death of Caesar, Cleopatra's position in Rome became uncertain. In his will, Caesar had proclaimed his great-nephew Octavian as his successor. Octavian was a young man of eighteen. There was no mention of Cleopatra or Caesarion. Soon after Caesar's death, the still-grieving Cleopatra left Rome with Caesarion and Ptolemy XIV and returned to Alexandria. Back in the capital of Egypt, she soon faced new problems that proved to be very difficult to solve.

THE REIGN
OF CLEOPATRA

As Cleopatra returned to Egypt, major conflicts were brewing for control of the Roman world. The queen tried to chart a careful path among the major contestants in the conflicts. Cleopatra hoped to keep her throne, avoid being conquered by Rome, and preserve the independence of her country.

 ## PROBLEMS IN EGYPT

When Cleopatra left Rome and arrived in Alexandria, her country was in the midst of another famine. Once again, the Nile flood levels had been very low. As a result, not enough grain could be grown to feed the Egyptian people. Shortly after Cleopatra came back, her brother Ptolemy XIV disappeared. An ancient Jewish historian, Josephus, believed that the queen murdered him. As Josephus wrote: "She had . . . poisoned her brother, because she knew that he was to be king of Egypt, and this when he was but fifteen years old . . . ."[1] Political murders were not unusual among the Ptolemies. This was a common method of eliminating opponents. Historian Michael Grant believes that Cleopatra may have murdered her brother because she feared that he might eventually challenge her right to the throne. In the past, her brother Ptolemy XIII and his advisors had driven her out of Alexandria. It is even possible that they were planning her murder. Cleopatra wanted to prevent this problem from arising again. In addition, the queen wanted to provide a place for her son, Caesarion. Shortly after her brother disappeared, Cleopatra declared her son Ptolemy XV.[2]

One of the ways that Cleopatra hoped to preserve her power and the independence of Egypt was to emphasize her connection with Julius Caesar. She had declared Caesarion as Caesar's son. Caesarion now provided a vital link with the past. Since he was only three years old, Caesarion was not a rival, like her fifteen-year-old brother, Ptolemy XIV, had been. On temples across Egypt, Cleopatra ordered that she and Caesarion should be represented as gods in wall paintings. Cleopatra was shown as Isis and Caesarion was portrayed as Horus, the god of the sky and the son of Isis and Osiris. By linking herself and her son to local Egyptian gods, Cleopatra may have gained more support from her people.

As Cleopatra was trying to strengthen her own position, the Roman world was being torn apart by conflict. Caesar had named his great-nephew Octavian heir to his power. But Mark Antony believed that he had proven himself an able leader and that he should have been given Caesar's authority instead.

This engraving shows the goddess Isis (left), the god Osiris (center), and their son Horus. Cleopatra identified herself with Isis and her son Caesarion with Horus.

 ## ANTONY'S EARLY CAREER

Mark Antony was born in Rome about 83 B.C. One of his grandfathers, also called Mark Antony, had been a famous orator and politician. In 100 B.C., the elder Antony was given command of a naval squadron in the Mediterranean. With this squadron, Mark Antony eliminated many of the pirates attacking Roman merchant ships. Three decades later, the elder Mark Antony's son, Marcus, also commanded a Roman force against the pirates. He fought them in Spain and in the eastern Mediterranean. But Marcus was far less successful than his father. Marcus died in 71 B.C., leaving behind his wife, Julia, and his young son, Mark Antony.

Mark Antony was raised primarily by his mother, Julia, a relative of Julius Caesar. As a young man, Antony spent much of his time drinking and gambling. He ran up huge debts, which he could not afford to repay. In 58 B.C., Antony left Rome to live in Greece, possibly to escape his debts. Here Antony studied public speaking and trained for a career in the army. Later that year, he joined the army of Gabinius. It was heading for the Roman province of Syria to deal with an uprising. Antony proved himself to be a natural soldier, leading attacks on fortified towns.

Once Gabinius had won the war in Syria, he headed to Egypt in 56 B.C. With him was Ptolemy Auletes, whom the Romans were planning to restore to the Egyptian throne. Antony won a decisive battle at Pelusium outside Alexandria. Auletes wanted him to kill the enemy captives, but Antony spared their lives. It was an act of mercy that Egyptians never forgot. During his tour of duty in Egypt, Antony may have first met Cleopatra. She would have been about thirteen years old.

After serving in Egypt, Antony went to Gaul. Once again, he proved to be a skillful leader and gradually became Caesar's most trusted officer. As his biographer Eleanor Goltz Huzar wrote:

> His character was that of a battlefield warrior—for good and ill. Courageous, bold, loyal to friends, chivalrous to enemies, he was at his best when the challenge was the

greatest and his slackest [laziest] at times of ease. . . . He was superbly intelligent . . . his talents chiefly in army tactics and in solving military problems. . . . He seemed born to be a second in command; and Caesar, who understood him fully, trusted him completely as a lieutenant. . . .[3]

Antony returned from Gaul and was elected to public office in Rome in 50 B.C. He represented Caesar's interests in the struggle against Pompey and the Senate. When Caesar crossed the Rubicon River with his legion to challenge Rome, Antony joined him. Later he commanded the left wing of Caesar's army at Pharsalus.

Antony was a powerfully built, handsome man. He was not only a favorite among his soldiers but very attractive to women. Antony was married several times. In 47 B.C., he married a woman named Fulvia. She was a beautiful, very powerful woman who tried to advance her husband's career in Rome.

TENSIONS BETWEEN ANTONY AND OCTAVIAN

After Caesar's death, Antony was disappointed with the dictator's will that named Octavian as his successor. Antony believed that he should have been named to succeed Caesar. Tensions began to develop almost immediately between Antony and Octavian. Many members of the Senate backed Octavian. They were led by the orator Cicero. He promoted the idea that Antony was unfit to take over Caesar's power. Open conflict broke out between Antony and Octavian. Both of them had raised their own armies. In 43 B.C., Antony's forces were defeated at Mutina in northern Italy. He fled to Gaul. Once Octavian was victorious, however, he found that Cicero and the Senate no longer supported him. They did not want another dictator. Instead the Senate wanted to restore the Roman Republic.

Indeed, about one-third of the Senate had left Rome to join Cassius and Brutus. They had fled from Rome after the assassination of Caesar. Cassius and Brutus then began raising an army in the east to restore the Roman Republic. Cassius was trying to take control of the Roman province of Syria. Facing him was a Roman army under the command of Publius Cornelius Dolabella. He was a strong supporter of Caesar and called on Cleopatra to support him. Roman legions still in Egypt since the time of Caesar marched north to join Dolabella, but he was defeated by Cassius in 43 B.C.

DEFEAT OF THE REPUBLICANS

Meanwhile, Octavian had decided to patch up his differences with Antony. Octavian needed Antony's support to defeat the Senate. Together with another Roman general, Lepidus, Antony and Octavian formed the Second Triumvirate in 43 B.C. Antony and Octavian then decided to pay back all the politicians in Rome who had opposed them. In a murderous bloodbath, Roman senators and other political leaders, including Cicero, were killed. Then Antony and Octavian turned their attention to the east.

After his victory in Syria, Cassius expected Cleopatra to support him, but the queen hesitated. She had no reason to support Cassius, who had murdered Julius Caesar. In addition, the Second Triumvirate had decided to support Caesarion as her coruler in Egypt. Cassius was furious. He had been able to gather support from other eastern provinces, but nothing came from Egypt. Cassius decided to invade Egypt. But before his army could move he had to deal with the Second Triumvirate. Octavian and Antony gathered their army together to defeat Brutus and Cassius who had increased the size of their forces. Finally, Antony and Octavian invaded northern Greece in 42 B.C. Cleopatra had tried to assist the Triumvirate, but her fleet had to turn back to Alexandria because of severe storms.

Battles broke out at Philippi, near the Aegean Sea. It was a gigantic clash that pitted two armies of about one hundred thousand men apiece. Octavian took little part in the battles because he was sick. But Antony led his troops to total victory. Both Brutus and Cassius killed themselves on the battlefield. As historian Eleanor Huzar wrote, "Antony . . . covered Brutus's body with his own purple cloak, honoring the man who had struggled to his death for the ideal of a republic which other men had already discarded."[4]

Antony and Cleopatra

After his victory at Philippi, Antony was considered the leading man in Rome. Many political leaders believed that Octavian had showed at Philippi that he was unfit to

Cicero and Cleopatra

Marcus Tullius Cicero was born in Arpinum, near Rome, in 106 B.C. As a young man, Cicero decided to become a lawyer. He studied law and became an experienced orator. By winning important legal cases, Cicero made a name for himself.

In 63 B.C., Cicero was elected consul. During his term of office, he put down a conspiracy to overthrow the Roman Republic. After Caesar, Pompey, and Crassus formed the First Triumvirate, they wanted Cicero's support. But he regarded the Triumvirate as a threat to the Roman Republic and refused to join them. As a result, Caesar's followers drove Cicero out of Rome in 58 B.C., and he lost all his property.

Eventually, the Triumvirate allowed Cicero to return to Rome. In a letter to his friend Atticus, Cicero wrote of his dislike for Cleopatra: "I hate the queen!" Apparently, she had promised to give him gifts that were never delivered. "And the Queen's insolence," Cicero continued, "I cannot recall without indignation. So no dealings with that lot. They seem to think I have not only no spirit, but no feelings at all."[5] With his speeches, Cicero unsuccessfully tried to prevent Octavian and Antony from taking control of Rome. As a result, Cicero was killed.

lead men in battle. Antony decided to leave Octavian in Rome and head east and south to govern the Roman provinces. Historian Michael Grant believes that Antony made this decision for several reasons. "One reason why he selected the east," Grant wrote, "was because of its immense wealth." Indeed, Egypt was one of the wealthiest of the provinces. "Moreover, in Roman eyes, one of the most pressing tasks of the future was to renew the war against the Parthians." Caesar had already decided to lead a campaign against them before he was assassinated. The Parthians still posed an enormous threat to the Roman eastern provinces.[6]

Antony went to Ephesus, located in present-day Turkey. He arrived in a brilliant procession, which included many dancers and musicians and proclaimed him as the New Dionysus, the god of wine. Antony had decided to associate himself with the most popular god

THE PARTHIANS

Parthia was located near the Caspian Sea. It had been conquered by Alexander the Great in the fourth century B.C. But about one hundred years later, the Parthians revolted and established their own empire. The Parthians were renowned for their cavalry, who were skilled archers and fierce fighters. When Marcus Crassus tried to conquer the Parthians, he was defeated in 53 B.C. Caesar had hoped to lead a successful campaign against the Parthians, but he was assassinated in 44 B.C. The Parthian Empire remained a powerful enemy of Rome.

in the east. After settling down in Ephesus, Antony called in the governors of the Roman provinces. He also wanted to meet with the monarchs who ruled small kingdoms allied with Rome. In order to strengthen relations in the east, he reduced taxes and improved trade. Antony also established military colonies by rewarding his soldiers with land. These colonies provided a permanent defense against any invasions.

Among the leaders Antony asked to meet at Ephesus was Cleopatra. At first she resisted, possibly to show her independence to the powerful Roman general. Then Cleopatra finally agreed to meet Antony at Tarsus, which was closer to Alexandria. The historian Plutarch described her entrance on the river Cydnus into Tarsus. She came "in a barge with a gilded stern and outspread sails of purple, while oars of silver beat time to the music of flutes and fifes and harps. She herself lay all alone under a canopy of cloth of gold, dressed as Venus in a picture, and beautiful young boys, like painted Cupids, stood on each side to fan her." Her entrance was designed to impress Antony and according to Plutarch it did and he was "captivated." As Plutarch put it, Cleopatra had reached a time of life "when women's beauty is most splendid and their intellects are in full maturity." They had dinner aboard Cleopatra's barge where Antony was dazzled by all the lights. Then, according to Plutarch, Antony no longer gave any thought to his wife Fulvia or his other duties. Instead he decided to accompany Cleopatra back to Alexandria.[7]

The facts, however, may have been somewhat different. Other historians believe that Antony and

Cleopatra were not only attracted to each other but were also two political leaders who needed each other's support. Cleopatra saw Antony as the most powerful man in the Mediterranean world. She believed that he was someone who could help her protect her kingdom. Antony recognized that Egypt was the richest area in the east. He wanted Cleopatra's support—money, supplies, and troops—for his war against the Parthians. The queen agreed to help Antony. In return, she wanted him to kill her half sister Arsinoe. Although Arsinoe had been taken to Rome as a captive by Caesar, she was allowed to leave after his death. Since that time, she had been plotting to overthrow Cleopatra. Antony immediately ordered her execution.[8]

Antony and Cleopatra traveled to Alexandria early in 40 B.C. Unlike Caesar who had brought soldiers with him, Antony entered alone. He was welcomed by the people of Alexandria, where he remained for the next few months. Plutarch wrote that Antony wasted time in huge banquets, drinking, and games. Cleopatra accompanied him in all his activities. "She played at dice with him," Plutarch wrote:

> drank with him, hunted with him; and when he exercised in arms [weapons], she was there to see. At night she would go rambling with him [in Alexandria] to disturb and torment people at their doors and windows, dressed like a servant-woman, for Antony also went in servant's disguise. . . . The Alexandrians in general liked it all well enough, and

A Fishing Trip

The Roman historian Plutarch tells this story about a day that Cleopatra and Antony went fishing:

> . . . his fishing must not be forgotten. He went out one day to angle with Cleopatra, and, being so unfortunate as to catch nothing in the presence of his mistress, he gave secret orders to the fishermen to dive under water, and put fishes that had been already taken upon his hooks; and these he drew so fast that the Egyptian perceived it. But, feigning great admiration, she told everybody how dexterous Antony was, and invited them next day to come and see him again. So, when a number of them had come on board the fishing-boats, as soon as he had let down his hook, one of her servants was beforehand with his divers and fixed upon his hook a salted fish from Pontus. Antony, feeling his line give, drew up the prey, and when, as may be imagined, great laughter ensued, "Leave," said Cleopatra, "the fishing-rod, general, to us poor sovereigns of Pharos and Canopus; your game is cities, provinces, and kingdoms."[9]

joined good-humoredly and kindly in his frolic and play. . . .[10]

ANTONY LEAVES ALEXANDRIA

Antony's vacation in Alexandria was cut short in the spring of 40 B.C. The Parthians had launched an attack on Syria. Meanwhile, Octavian's power was growing in Rome. Antony's wife, Fulvia, had led a rebellion against Octavian, but she had been defeated and left Italy. Antony met Fulvia at Athens, Greece. There he criticized her for trying to upset his alliance with Octavian. Antony traveled west to Rome, leaving Fulvia in Athens. She died shortly afterward.

Although he may have been attracted to Cleopatra, Antony did not hesitate to leave Alexandria. Antony realized that he needed to remain Octavian's ally. As historian Eleanor Huzar wrote, "Antony was ruled by his head, not his heart."[11] Antony and Octavian decided to continue their alliance. Neither of them was strong enough to defeat the other one. In fact, Antony married Octavian's sister, Octavia, in 40 B.C. She was a beautiful, intelligent woman who helped bind her brother and her husband together.

CLEOPATRA GUIDES EGYPT'S FUTURE

Antony and his new wife, Octavia, went to Athens, Greece. From Athens, Antony ruled the Roman provinces of the East. Meanwhile, Cleopatra remained in Alexandria. In 40 B.C., she gave birth to twins. She

Born in 63 B.C., Octavian was the son of Gaius Octavius. Octavius was married to Atia, Julius Caesar's niece.

During the war with Pompey, Octavian supported his great uncle Julius Caesar. He traveled to Spain in 45 B.C. There Caesar's forces defeated an army commanded by Pompey's sons. Early in 44 B.C., Caesar selected Octavian for political office as "master of the horse." Octavian traveled east, where he heard about his great uncle's assassination. Caesar had named Octavian as his heir. But, according to the historian Suetonius, Octavian

> hesitated for some time whether he should call to his aid the legions stationed in the neighborhood; but he abandoned the design as rash and premature. However, returning to Rome [as a private citizen], he took possession of his inheritance, although his mother was apprehensive that such a measure might be attended with danger. . . .[12]

Octavian now began calling himself Julius Caesar Octavianus, because he had been adopted by Caesar in his will. Although he was only eighteen years old, Octavian had the advantage of being named by Caesar to succeed him. Therefore, Octavian decided to make a bid for power, and was backed by many units in the army.

named the boy Alexander Helios [the sun] and the girl Cleopatra Selene [the moon]. Mark Antony was the father of the children.

During the next three years, Antony ruled the eastern Roman Empire from Athens. While Antony remained in Athens, the Parthians began an invasion of the eastern provinces. They quickly took control of Syria. Then they turned south and conquered the kingdom of Judaea. They removed the Judaean king, Hyrcanus II, and killed one of his sons. The Parthians also drove the other son, Herod, out of the kingdom. He fled to Egypt, looking for support from Cleopatra.

Cleopatra and Herod had an uneasy relationship. In the past, Judaea had been part of the Egyptian empire. Cleopatra wanted to take control of it again. Judaea was

Cleopatra wanted to acquire more lands where dates were grown. Here, a modern Egyptian man sits beneath a date palm.

a rich source of dates, a natural sweetener for many foods in the ancient world. Fragrant balsam shrubs were also grown there, producing a substance that was widely used in ancient times in perfumes and medicines. When the Parthians invaded Judaea, Herod sought protection in Egypt. At this point, there was little that Cleopatra could do to defeat the Parthians and take Judaea for herself. Therefore, she entertained Herod and arranged for him to take a ship to Rome. In Rome, Herod won over Octavian's support to retake Judaea from the Parthians. In addition, Herod had impressed Antony as a capable ruler when they had met earlier in the East, so Antony agreed to help Herod regain control of Judaea.

 ## WAR AGAINST THE PARTHIANS

In order to help Herod and reassert Roman power in the east, Antony had to defeat the Parthians. This required a large, well-supplied army. In 37 B.C., Antony and Octavian met in Tarentum, Italy. They needed to figure out how to safeguard the empire. There was still friction between the two leaders. Both men were competing to determine who would be the most powerful. However, Octavia may have helped Antony and Octavian patch up their differences. As a result, they decided to continue the Second Triumvirate.

Octavian needed men for his campaigns to safeguard the western part of the empire. However, he promised to send Antony an additional twenty thousand soldiers for his campaign against the Parthians. Antony left Tarentum to prepare for his campaign, but the troops

HEROD THE GREAT

Born in 73 B.C., Herod was the son of Antipater. He was a close advisor of Hyrcanus, king of Judaea. With support from Rome, Antipater had his two sons appointed governors in Judaea. At age twenty-five, Herod became governor of Galilee. Following Caesar's death, Cassius tried to raise troops in Judaea. He forced Antipater to raise money among the Jews in Judaea to support a Roman army. Many Jews resented Antipater, who was assassinated in 43 B.C.

Shortly afterward, Herod married Mariamne, the granddaughter of Hyrcanus. This helped secure Herod's position as a successor to Hyrcanus. Nevertheless, in 40 B.C., Hyrcanus was driven out of Judaea by the Parthians. Herod was forced to flee Judaea for Egypt and later Rome. He returned in 38 B.C., with the help of Antony and a Roman army, to defeat the Parthians. Although Antony supported Herod's position in Jerusalem, Cleopatra wanted him removed. The historian Josephus claimed that Antony "would not always hearken to her to do those flagrant enormities she would have persuaded him to. . . ."[13] Antony agreed to give Cleopatra parts of Judaea, but not the entire country. Herod remained King of Judaea until his death in 4 B.C.

did not arrive. About this time, he sent a message to Cleopatra. Antony asked her to come to Antioch for a meeting. He hoped to persuade her to help him. Antony wanted Cleopatra to provide the additional men and supplies for the coming campaign against the Parthians. In return for helping him, Antony agreed to expand the Egyptian empire. Antony gave Cleopatra Phoenicia, located along the coast of the Mediterranean Sea near present-day Lebanon. He also decided that the large island of Cyprus should become part of Egypt.

According to historian Mary Hamer, new coins began appearing in Egypt around this time. These bore portraits of Antony and Cleopatra, one on each side of a coin. The queen appears as "an older woman wearing a big necklace. The nose is big, the lower jaw sticks out. . . . Cleopatra looks like Mark Antony in a wig. Other coins show portraits of Antony and Cleopatra next to each other on one side."[14]

Cleopatra also wanted control of neighboring Judaea. By this time, the Romans had driven the Parthians out of Judaea and made Herod king. Antony refused to remove Herod as Cleopatra wanted. However, he did give her control of the areas in Judaea that were sources of dates and balsam. In addition, she received territory along the Red Sea, east of Egypt.

 THE INVASION OF PARTHIA

According to historian Jack Lindsay, Cleopatra did not believe that Parthia was the main danger facing Antony. She believed that "Octavian was the main enemy who must be faced and dealt with sooner or later, and the sooner the better; what needed to be done was to organize for the final confrontation; when Octavian was defeated, everything was possible and Parthia could be easily subdued." However, Cleopatra did not realize that many Romans hated her. They also distrusted Antony because of his relationship with Cleopatra. He reasoned that if he could defeat the Parthians, then the Romans would recognize his true value to the empire.[15]

In late spring, 36 B.C., Antony began the invasion of Parthia. He hoped to accomplish what Caesar had been unable to achieve. A victory over the Parthians would make him the most successful military leader in Rome. Antony led a huge army, possibly one hundred thousand infantry and cavalry.[16] The Parthians did not risk a battle with such a large force. Instead, they attacked small parts of Antony's army as it marched north. Antony's supply carts and his equipment for laying siege to the Parthian cities moved very slowly. It fell behind the main army. The small force guarding these supplies was struck by the Parthians and completely destroyed. As a result, Antony's campaign was seriously undercut. Antony had no choice but to turn around and head south.

As his army retreated, it was struck by constant hit-and-run attacks from the Parthians. Antony's troops made very slow progress. The men suffered from cold and hunger. Nevertheless, they continued to support Antony. He shared all the hardships of the retreat with his men. As Plutarch wrote, there was:

the unanimous feeling amongst small and great alike, officers and common soldiers, to prefer his good opinion of them to their very lives and being. . . . For this devotion . . . there were many reasons . . . his eloquence, his frank and open manners . . . his familiarity in talking with everybody, and, at this time particularly, his kindness in visiting and pitying the sick, joining in all their pains, and furnishing them with all things necessary, so that the sick and wounded were even more eager to serve than those that were whole and strong.[17]

Eventually, the ragged army reached Syria, where it had started. By the end of Antony's campaign, an estimated 40 percent of his troops had died.[18] The war against the Parthians had been a disaster. Antony left the army in Syria to travel southward for a reunion with Cleopatra in Phoenicia. He needed her emotional support as well as more supplies to renew the campaign.[19] They met each other early in 35 B.C. By this time, Cleopatra had given birth to the couple's third child—Ptolemy Philadelphus.

A NEW CAMPAIGN

While Antony spent time with Cleopatra, his wife, Octavia, had come to Athens from Rome, bringing supplies and a few troops. However, Octavian had not sent the twenty thousand soldiers he had promised earlier. Antony refused to see his wife. He sent a messenger, telling her to leave the men and supplies that she had brought and return to Rome. The Romans were scandalized by Antony's behavior.[20] According to

CLEOPATRA ON COINS

The coins of Cleopatra's reign bore the images of the queen. Archeologists have discovered some of these coins, including a silver drachma, from about 47 B.C., which shows a young queen with an "almost smiling expression and large eyes, a strong hooked nose and prominent chin," according to historian Susan Walker. Walker goes on to describe Cleopatra:

> Her hair is drawn back from the face in conventional braids termed . . . melon hairstyle, after the resemblance of the divided braids to the segments of a melon. Some curls escape behind the ears and a small knot of hair appears to have been coiled above the brow. The braids are confined beneath a broad diadem [crown], and bound into a bun at the nape of the neck.[21]

Cleopatra's image also appeared on bronze drachmas. Sculptures of a woman's head—perhaps Cleopatra's—have been found in Rome. This was during the period when she traveled there to see Caesar. Coins issued in Egypt during the period when she was with Mark Antony show images of both Antony and Cleopatra. Again she is portrayed with a hooked nose and a sharp chin and jaw. Marble statues of Cleopatra have also been found in Egypt. They show her with a hairstyle and face similar to those on the early coins.

historian Michel Chauveau, Octavian may have planned for this to happen. He knew that Antony would not be happy with the few soldiers that had been sent to him. Nevertheless, Antony lost many of his supporters in Rome. Meanwhile, Octavia returned home and continued to live in Rome without criticizing Antony. This behavior won her support among the Romans.[22]

Plutarch claimed that Antony's decision was due entirely to Cleopatra. She did not want him to go back to his wife:

> . . . she feigned [pretended] to be dying for love of Antony, bringing her body down by slender diet; when he entered the room, she fixed her eyes upon him in a rapture, and when he left, seemed to . . . half faint away. She took great pains that he should see her in tears, and, as soon as he noticed it, hastily dried them up and turned away, as if it were her wish that he should know nothing of it.[23]

THE DONATIONS OF ALEXANDRIA

Antony remained in the east. He lived with Cleopatra in Alexandria, and built up his army once again. Instead of embarking on a new campaign against the Parthians, he attacked Armenia. This country is located north and east of present-day Syria and Turkey. Antony blamed the Armenians for not giving him all the support they had promised during the Parthian campaign. Cleopatra supported the invasion. According to Jack Lindsay, "Since her plans involved the mustering of the eastern world against Rome, it would never do to leave such a traitor secure in the rear, destroying the Asian unity she wanted. So both she and Antony agreed that first of all they must deal with Armenia."[24] In a quick campaign during 34 B.C., Armenia was easily conquered.

Following his victory in Armenia, Antony returned to Alexandria. He and Cleopatra staged a huge celebration, known as the Donations of Alexandria. Antony and Cleopatra sat on huge thrones at the Gymnasium in Alexandria. Cleopatra was portrayed as the goddess Isis and Antony as Osiris and Dionysus. Their children also attended the celebration. Young Alexander Helios became the new king of Armenia. Ptolemy Philadelphus was made ruler of Syria. Young Cleopatra Selene became queen of North Africa. Cleopatra was proclaimed Queen of Kings.

The old empire of the Ptolemies had been restored, under the direction of Antony and the Romans. Cleopatra had taken her place among the great rulers of the world—thanks to her relationship with Antony. Cleopatra and Antony were creating a new empire in the east. But this empire produced resentment among Octavian and the people of Rome. Soon this resentment would lead to open warfare.

7

A Decision at Actium

In 31 B.C., Octavian's army clashed with the forces of Antony and Cleopatra at Actium, on the west coast of Greece. Cleopatra's future and the fate of her empire rested on the outcome of the battle.

Conflict between Antony and Octavian

Following the Donations of Alexandria, the conflict between Antony and Octavian grew worse. Octavian was very angry that Antony had given any territory to Cleopatra. He portrayed Antony as being under the influence of Cleopatra—doing whatever she told him to do. Antony's actions also displeased many people in Rome, who thought that Antony had given away territory that rightly belonged to the Roman Empire. Octavian played on these feelings in his own propaganda. He accused Antony of allying himself with Cleopatra. Since Antony was not in Rome, it was difficult for him to defend himself. Many Romans also feared that somehow Cleopatra might gain control of the

Roman empire. Indeed Cleopatra was widely quoted as saying that she would "dispense justice on the Capitol." In other words, Cleopatra thought that she would rule from Rome.[1]

Writing about this time, the Roman poet Virgil described Cleopatra this way:

> *What of that woman, she whose charms*
> *Brought scandal on the Roman arms,*
> *And strumpet [bad woman] to her very thralls*
> *Aspired to pass the Roman walls*
> *And rule our Senate, as the fee*
> *Due from her lover's lechery?*[2]

In turn, Antony's supporters criticized Octavian. They said he was an incompetent general. They also reminded Romans that it was Antony, not Octavian, who had won the battle of Philippi. Meanwhile, Antony did everything he could to win over influential members of the Roman Senate. He even asked for their approval of the Donations of Alexandria.

By the end of 33 B.C., Octavian announced that the Triumvirate was dissolved. Some Roman senators did not support Octavian's decision. Early the following year, about three hundred senators—approximately one third of the Senate—left Rome. They joined Antony and Cleopatra in Ephesus. There they found that Antony had assembled a huge army. His forces included about one hundred thousand infantry and approximately twelve thousand cavalry. In addition, Antony had the support of a huge navy, including five hundred warships.

Approximately two hundred of them had been supplied by Cleopatra.[3]

At Ephesus, according to modern historian Edith Flamarion, Cleopatra

> . . . appeared publicly as queen, escorted by Roman soldiers carrying shields bearing her [insignias]. With Antony at her side, she dispensed justice, presided over meetings, and reviewed the troops. She could be seen traveling across the city on horseback—or on a litter that, according to rumor, Antony sometimes followed on foot. Like all conquerors, she plundered the wealth of the region in order to send it to Alexandria . . . [including] many statues and art objects. . . .

In addition, Antony gave her two hundred thousand books from a large library at Pergamum in Asia Minor. These were shipped off to the Library at Alexandria. All of these acts did not win her any friends among Antony's Roman officers or the members of the Senate who had joined him.[4]

Meanwhile Octavian was preparing for the coming battle by raising an army in Italy. In order to pay for the troops, Octavian was forced to levy heavy taxes on Roman citizens. They were required to pay as much as twenty-five percent of their income to the Roman government.[5] This angered many Romans. However, the money enabled Octavian to raise an army about the same size as Antony's.

Plutarch criticized Antony's strategy. He said that Antony should have invaded Rome while many citizens were angry at Octavian and he was still trying to gather his army. As Plutarch wrote, "this is looked upon as one of the greatest of Antony's oversights, that he did not then press the war. For he allowed time at once for [Octavian] to make his preparations and for the commotions to pass over. For while people were having their money called for, they were mutinous and violent; but, having paid it, they held their peace."[6]

But Antony may have had little choice. He realized that many Romans were suspicious of Cleopatra. If she accompanied him on an invasion, it might look as if the Egyptian queen were about to take control of Rome. Indeed, some of Antony's advisors tried to persuade him to send Cleopatra back to Egypt. They felt that she was undermining Antony's war efforts. However, Cleopatra wanted to remain part of the military campaign. Antony was reluctant to oppose her. She had provided almost half of his navy. In addition, she turned over a huge treasure, worth about twenty thousand talents. This money helped Antony pay his troops.[7]

OCTAVIAN'S PREPARATIONS FOR WAR

Some senators who had joined Antony became so upset with him that they decided to return to Rome. They brought word to Octavian that Antony had left his will in Rome. He had deposited the will at the temple of the Vestal Virgins. These were a group of highly respected women in Rome. The Vestal Virgins were among the leaders of the Roman religion. Octavian broke into their temple and took Antony's will. Then Octavian published what he claimed were important parts of the will.

According to the will, Antony gave much of his lands to Cleopatra. He wanted to be buried in Alexandria alongside of her. As the historian Cassius Dio wrote,

> This caused the Romans in their indignation to believe . . . that if Antony should prevail, he would bestow their city upon Cleopatra and transfer the seat of power to Egypt. And they became so angry at this that all, not only Antony's enemies or those who were not siding with either man, but even his most intimate friends, censured [criticized] him severely. . . . [8]

Octavian had turned Antony's will into an effective piece of propaganda. Nevertheless, Octavian realized that the Roman people still regarded Antony as a courageous general. However, as Cassius Dio put it, they thought that Cleopatra "had enslaved him. . . ."[9] Therefore, late in 32 B.C., Octavian declared war on Cleopatra. This focused the anger of the Roman people on Cleopatra instead of Antony.

CLEOPATRA AND ANTONY PREPARE FOR BATTLE

By this time, Antony and Cleopatra had moved their headquarters to Samos, an island in the Aegean Sea. There they held huge celebrations, which were a tribute to the god Dionysus. From Samos, Cleopatra and Antony moved to Athens, in southern Greece. From this position, Antony's ships could protect his supply routes to Egypt. Antony relied on Egyptian wheat to feed his soldiers. In Athens, Antony also announced that he was divorcing Octavia. This left him free to marry Cleopatra. However, Antony's advisors continued to urge him to send Cleopatra back to Egypt, and some of these advisors even deserted Antony. As historian Jack Lindsay wrote: "Many men were painfully swayed between a genuine admiration for Antony and a conviction that by supporting him they were betraying Roman ideals in unforgivable ways." In other words, they seemed to support Cleopatra and Egypt instead of the future of the Roman Empire.[10]

Some of Antony's friends in Rome finally sent an ambassador, named Geminius, to plead with Antony to dismiss Cleopatra. Geminius came to beg Antony "to take heed and not allow himself to be deprived by vote of his authority [leadership in the Roman Empire] and proclaimed a public enemy to the Roman state. But Geminius no sooner arrived in Greece but he was looked upon as one of Octavia's spies." According to Plutarch, Geminius was not given a place of honor at Antony's table. Nevertheless, Geminius finally spoke to Antony and urged him to send Cleopatra back to Egypt. When Antony became angry at such a suggestion, Geminius returned to Rome.[11]

By the winter of 32–31 B.C., Antony and Cleopatra had moved their headquarters north to Patrae, a Greek city on the Gulf of Corinth. Antony had also set up outposts as far north as the island of Corcyra. He occupied other islands in the Ionian Sea, west of Greece. These outposts enabled him to spot Octavian's army when it finally left Rome and sailed for Greece.

In spring 31 B.C., Octavian began his invasion of Greece. Before his army began to move, he sent his admiral, Marcus Agrippa, ahead with part of the fleet. Octavian's navy numbered about four hundred warships. Agrippa caught Antony off guard. In March, he captured one of Antony's outposts at Methone in southern Greece. From this position, Agrippa sent out his ships to capture other islands, threatening Antony's supply route from Egypt. Few ships could get through to Antony's

MARCUS VIPSANIUS AGRIPPA

Born in 63 B.C., Agrippa was about the same age as Octavian. Indeed, the two young men had known each other as students. After the death of Caesar in 44 B.C., Agrippa helped Octavian put down the revolt of Fulvia, the first wife of Mark Antony. Later, in 37 B.C., Agrippa became consul in Rome. Meanwhile, he had also become a very successful naval commander. Agrippa trained his crews and prepared his fleet so well that in 36 B.C. they defeated Pompey's son, Sextus Pompeius, who had been menacing Rome and threatening Octavian's rule. In the contest against Antony, Agrippa built smaller, faster ships. They were more maneuverable than the Egyptian warships. These ships helped Agrippa win the Battle of Actium in 31 B.C. After Octavian took control of the Roman Empire, Agrippa helped him put down a revolt in Spain. Later, he served as governor of Syria. Agrippa died in 12 B.C.

army. Indeed, his troops were forced to collect what supplies they could find in Greece.

While Antony was pre-occupied with Agrippa, Octavian transported his troops from Italy to northern Greece. Octavian's army moved rapidly south. They took up a position on a Greek peninsula. Just across the water, Antony's army was camped at Actium. Antony's soldiers guarded the entrance to a large harbor. Inside, his fleet lay at anchor. Outside the harbor, in the Ionian Sea, Octavian's ships patrolled the area. Commanded by Agrippa, they blockaded Antony's navy inside the Actium harbor.

Suddenly, Antony and Cleopatra found themselves trapped at Actium.

THE BATTLE OF ACTIUM

As Antony's army and navy sat at Actium, their situation grew worse. The army was struck by disease. Actium is a low-lying area that is prone to malaria. This often fatal disease is carried by mosquitoes. Part of Antony's navy was outside of Actium, guarding the outposts in the Aegean Sea. Other ships at Actium could not be manned because Antony could not find enough rowers. This left him with only about three hundred ships in the harbor, ready to fight against Agrippa, which meant he was outnumbered by Agrippa's four-hundred-warship navy. Antony was stuck at Actium. Meanwhile, Agrippa had been picking off more of Antony's outposts in the south of Greece. As a result, Antony and Cleopatra found their escape blocked by the Roman Navy from the north as well as the south.

In August, during the hot summer in Greece, Antony's army tried to break out of Actium. He sent part of his army north around Octavian's position toward Macedonia. At the same time, the fleet tried to leave the harbor under cover of fog. Nevertheless, Agrippa's ships blocked Antony's fleet. It was forced to return to the harbor. At this point, Antony called a meeting of his generals to decide how to deal with Octavian. Some of them advised him to take his army into eastern Greece and abandon the huge fleet in the harbor. After all, they said, Antony was a victorious general who knew how to fight a land battle, not a contest at sea. Eventually, his generals argued, Octavian would be forced to follow, and Antony could then win a major victory.

But Cleopatra was opposed to this idea. She had helped assemble the fleet. As a result, she did not want to see it left to the mercy of Octavian and Agrippa. She recommended that Antony put some of his men onto the ships. Then they could try to break through the blockade. After the breakthrough, Cleopatra, with some of the Egyptian ships and her huge treasure, could slip out of Actium. Then she would sail for Egypt. Antony could follow with any of his own ships that could succeed in escaping the blockade.

Antony decided to follow Cleopatra's advice. He burned those vessels that did not have enough rowers to power them. Then he packed sails onto some of the other ships. The winds outside the harbor blew from

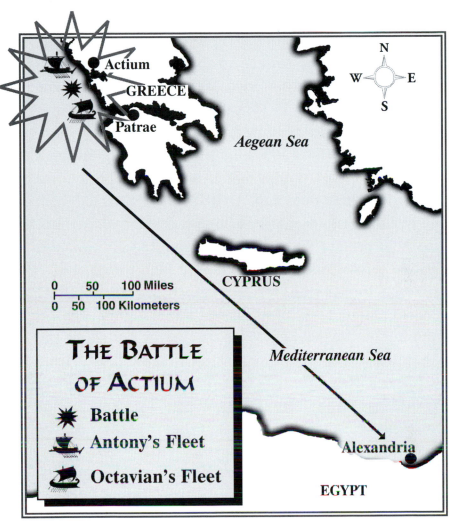

The Battle of Actium

- ✸ Battle
- ⛵ Antony's Fleet
- ⛵ Octavian's Fleet

Actium
GREECE
Patrae
Aegean Sea
CYPRUS
Mediterranean Sea
Alexandria
EGYPT

At the Battle of Actium, Mark Antony and Cleopatra's ships were trapped in their harbor by Octavian's large Roman fleet. They ended up having to flee to Alexandria, which was hundreds of miles away.

north to south in the afternoons. These winds would help his ships get past the blockade and sail toward Egypt.

Antony loaded twenty thousand members of the Roman legions onto the warships. These ships were huge crafts with wooden towers on them. Archers placed in the towers were expected to fire their arrows at the enemy during the battle. The ships also carried catapults. These war engines fired large rocks toward enemy ships, damaging the ships and killing the crewmen. Antony's ships, as well as Agrippa's, had long battering rams on the front. These were tipped with metal. This made them particularly effective at punching holes in enemy ships. To help protect their ships, Agrippa and Antony also reinforced the wooden sides of their hulls with metal.

On the morning of September 2, Antony's fleet began preparing to leave the harbor at Actium. He did not sail out immediately. Instead Antony waited for the afternoon breeze to begin blowing from the north. As he left the harbor, Antony's line of ships began to spread apart, leaving the center almost open. Agrippa's ships responded, also opening up the center of their line. On the flanks, the ships began to battle each other. Agrippa's ships were smaller and faster than Antony's. Several of them surrounded each of Antony's ships. Agrippa's men hurled javelins and fired arrows at the enemy soldiers on board. Agrippa's ships rammed the enemy. Meanwhile, his crews tried to throw grappling hooks onto Antony's ships, tying them together. Then Agrippa's troops boarded the enemy ships. In this way, twelve of Antony's ships were captured early in the battle.[12]

While the battle was under way, Cleopatra began to make her dash out of the harbor. With sixty ships, she headed through the open center of the two lines and headed south. Antony escaped from the battle with about forty of his ships.

The historian Plutarch criticized Antony for leaving the battle:

> Here it was that Antony showed to all the world that he was no longer actuated by the thoughts and motives of a commander or a man, or indeed by his own judgment at all. . . . For, as if he had been born part of her [Cleopatra], and must move with her wheresoever she went, as soon as he saw her ship sailing away, he abandoned all that were fighting and spending their lives for him, and put himself aboard a galley. . . .[13]

The battle continued until dark. Then, the rest of Antony's fleet surrendered to Octavian. However, Antony and Cleopatra had escaped. They still commanded one hundred ships and more than twenty thousand men.

The poet Virgil later wrote about the Battle of Actium. He described the victory of Octavian, who became known as Caesar Augustus.

> . . . There was Augustus
> Leading the Italians into battle, the whole Senate
> And people behind him, and the . . . Gods. . . .
> Twin flames played around his joyous brow, the Star
> Of his Father dawned above his head. Elsewhere
> Agrippa, with the aids of winds and gods,
> Towering led his line, and on his brows,

A proud war-emblem, gleamed the naval crown
Embellished with its replicas of ships' rams.
Opposing them was Antony backed by the riches
Of all East and nations' arms,
A conqueror from the far East and the shores
Of the red sea, enlisting with him Egypt
And the strength of the Orient and the farthest limits
Of Bactria [present-day Afghanistan] and—shame!—
his Egyptian spouse.[14]

Antony and Cleopatra had escaped with some of the fleet and a large treasure. This would enable them to fight again. Nevertheless, Antony was forced to admit that he had suffered a major defeat. On the ship carrying Antony south to southern Greece, he sat quietly, feeling very upset. As historian Eleanor Huzar wrote,

> During the three days' sail, Antony sat alone at the prow of his ship, brooding about the losses of his men, his ships, his reputation, his career as Caesar's successor to the Roman Empire. As general, he knew the magnitude of his defeat; as man, he was shattered by the disaster.[15]

Antony had given the army instructions to leave Actium and head east. Instead, the legions realized that the war had been lost and so they negotiated with Octavian to join his army. Throughout the east, kings who had supported Antony changed sides and supported Octavian. Among them was Herod, who met Octavian on the island of Rhodes in the eastern Mediterranean and swore loyalty to him. According to the historian Josephus, Herod admitted that he had been a friend of Antony's. Herod even told Octavian that he had sent him money and supplies. The king also said that he had advised Antony to kill Cleopatra and continue to rule alone in the east. "By this speech," Josephus wrote, "and by his behavior, which showed the frankness of his mind, [Herod] greatly gained upon him [and] procured his [Octavian's] good will." As a result, Herod remained king of Judaea.[16]

CLEOPATRA AND ANTONY IN ALEXANDRIA

Cleopatra and Antony returned to Alexandria. Both realized that it was only a matter of time before Octavian headed south to invade Egypt. He wanted the vast treasure that Cleopatra had taken with her from Actium. In addition, Octavian wanted to eliminate both Antony and Cleopatra. They were his rivals as leaders of the Roman Empire. But before Octavian could march into Egypt, he had to deal with rebellions in other parts of his vast empire.

Meanwhile, Antony's defeats had left him "a broken man. He knew now that he had no chance against Octavian, and he lost all taste for the conflict," according to historian Jack Lindsay. "Not so Cleopatra. She meant to fight till the end and never admit defeat."[17]

Cleopatra began making plans for the future. One alternative was for her to escape from Egypt. She ordered ships to be built on the Red Sea. Cleopatra hoped that she might take her treasure aboard these ships and sail east to India. Egypt and India had traded for many years. However, these ships were burned by allies of Octavian from Petra (in present-day Jordan).[18]

Antony, however, was far too depressed to think about the future. With no Roman army or navy, he believed that there was little he could do to stop Octavian. Instead, Antony chose to spend much of the time alone in a small house near the Pharos Lighthouse.[19] Finally, he decided to join Cleopatra. They both participated in lavish parties at her palace in Alexandria.

In the meantime, during the summer of 30 B.C., Octavian's army approached the city and Cleopatra sent him a message. She offered to leave the throne if he would let one of her children reign. She received no response from Octavian and his army kept advancing. Cleopatra tried to defend the city of Pelusium to the east of Alexandria. But it fell to Octavian. As Octavian entered the city, Cleopatra had her treasure moved to a large stone building. Inside she placed the treasure along with enough firewood to burn everything. Octavian was afraid that she might destroy the treasure. Therefore, he sent Cleopatra letters saying that he might negotiate with her if she gave him the treasure.[20]

As Octavian's troops approached Alexandria, they heard strange sounds. According to Plutarch:

> . . . on a sudden was heard the sound of all sorts of instru-
> ments, and voices singing in tune, and the cry of a crowd
> of people shouting and dancing. . . . This tumultuous
> procession seemed to take its course right through the
> middle of the city to the gate nearest the enemy; here it
> became the loudest, and suddenly passed out. People

who reflected considered this to signify that [Dionysus] the god whom Antony had always made it his study to copy and imitate, had now forsaken him.[21]

Indeed, Antony also found himself deserted by his troops, who had decided to join Octavian. Antony offered to meet Octavian in a single, hand-to-hand combat to decide the fate of the empire, but Octavian refused. By August 1, 30 B.C., Octavian had taken control of Alexandria. Antony heard that Cleopatra was dead and decided that the time had also come to end his life. He asked his servant Eros to kill him, but instead Eros killed himself. Therefore Antony thrust a dagger into his own stomach. Just a moment later, Cleopatra's secretary entered to tell Antony that the queen was still alive.

Antony did not die immediately. Instead he was taken to the large building where Cleopatra had stored her treasure. She had locked herself inside along with some of her servants. Since the doors were shut, Antony was hoisted up into the building through a window. There he died beside Cleopatra.

Octavian was still afraid that Cleopatra might destroy her huge treasure. So he sent one of his advisors to negotiate with her. Gaius Proculeius was a friend of Antony's. Therefore, Cleopatra decided to open the door and speak to him. Having spotted a window up above, Proculeius returned later with some of Octavian's men. While one man spoke to Cleopatra, Proculeius and his servants went up through the window and captured the queen.

Mark Antony died at Cleopatra's side.

Cleopatra was taken to her palace where she met Octavian. Now that he had obtained her treasure, there was no reason to keep her alive. However, if Octavian executed Cleopatra, it might seem too brutal to many of her supporters. Therefore, Octavian let Cleopatra know that he planned to take her to Rome. In Rome, she would be paraded in front of the people as a prisoner. He believed that she would never submit to being humiliated in front of the Roman people, and he was right.

DEATH OF A QUEEN

In August, 30 B.C., Cleopatra, Queen of Egypt, committed suicide. Cleopatra had spent much of her life battling for the greatest prizes in the ancient world. One of those prizes was safeguarding her own country, Egypt. It was the richest country in the Mediterranean world. Together with the Roman general Mark Antony, Cleopatra also tried to win a second prize. It was even greater than the first. This prize was control of the Roman Empire. When Antony and Cleopatra were defeated by Octavian, she then faced a difficult choice. Cleopatra believed that she must choose between being taken to Rome as a captive and committing suicide.

Cleopatra chose suicide. Before she died, Octavian sent one of his staff to see her. Publius Cornelius Dolabella was a friend of Cleopatra's. He told her that Octavian was going back to Rome in a few days. The Roman leader, according to Dolabella, planned to take

Cleopatra and her children with him. She would be forced by Octavian to walk in a victory parade, celebrating his triumph over Antony and Cleopatra. Cleopatra's family, the Ptolemies, had been rulers in Egypt for three hundred years. She had no intention of humiliating herself by going to Rome and being jeered by the Roman people.

Octavian may have guessed the choice Cleopatra would make when he sent Dolabella to her. Indeed, one of her guards had been given secret orders by the Roman leader. He was told to let Cleopatra commit suicide rather than be taken to Italy. Octavian may have wanted Cleopatra to die. He did not wish to have a rival in Alexandria as he took over the vast Roman Empire. Cleopatra might become the center of revolts against him. However, he did not want to order her execution. The Roman people would not have supported Octavian if he had executed a woman. So Octavian may have created a situation that left Cleopatra no choice but to commit suicide.[22]

Cleopatra had tried to avoid this fate. When Octavian entered Alexandria, she tried to win him over. According to the Roman historian Cassius Dio (155–235 A.D.), Cleopatra tried to flirt with Octavian and capture him with her charms. As the historian wrote:

> . . . sweet were the glances she cast at him and the words she murmured to him. Now [Octavian] was not insensible to the ardor of her speech and the appeal to his passions, but he pretended to be; and letting his eyes rest upon the ground, he merely said: "Be of good cheer, woman, and keep a stout heart; for you shall suffer no

harm." She was greatly distressed . . . she said with an outburst of sobbing: "I neither wish to live nor can I live. . . . But this favor I beg of you . . . I may also die with Antony. . . ."[23]

Octavian had no desire to deny Cleopatra her last wish. She was a powerful ruler. Before she died, Cleopatra asked to make one final visit to the tomb of Mark Antony in Alexandria. Around August 12, 30 B.C., the queen sent a letter to Octavian. In the letter, she asked Octavian to allow her body to be placed beside Antony's. At this point, Octavian knew that Cleopatra was already carrying out plans for her own death.

 ## THE DEATH SCENE

The suicide of Cleopatra was first described by the ancient historian Plutarch, writing over a century later. Plutarch described the queen's death this way:

> And a country fellow brought her a little basket, which the guards intercepting and asking what it was, the fellow put the leaves which lay uppermost aside, and showed them it was full of figs. . . . Some relate that an asp [snake] was brought in amongst those figs and covered with the leaves, and that Cleopatra had arranged that it might settle on her before she knew, but, when she took away some of the figs and saw it, she said, "So here it is," and held out her bare arm to be bitten. Others say that it was kept in a vase, and that she vexed [angered] and pricked it with a golden spindle [needle] till it seized her arm. But what really took place is known to no one, since it was also said that she carried poison in a hollow bodkin

[a hair ornament shaped like a dagger], about which she wound her hair; yet there was not so much as a spot found, or any symptom of poison upon her body, nor was the asp seen within the [palace]. . . . Some relate that two faint puncture marks were found on Cleopatra's arm. . . . Such are the various accounts.[24]

When the guards entered Cleopatra's room, she had already died from the bite of the snake. The guards found two of her female servants. One was dying while the other was about to commit suicide. When one of the guards asked what had happened, and whether this was "well done of your lady," the servant answered: "Extremely well and as became the descendant of so many kings."[25]

The asp was probably an Egyptian cobra. These reptiles lived along the Nile River. According to historian Michael Foss, the bite "was not painful and death . . . was quick, perhaps within thirty minutes."[26] In fact, convicted criminals were regularly executed this way. Supposedly, it was less painful than being beheaded. The snake was a centuries-old symbol in Egypt. Statues of the pharaohs traditionally featured a snake in the ruler's crown.

Ancient historians, however, disagreed about how many snakes were brought into the palace in the basket of figs. The poet Horace wrote that there was more than one asp. Indeed statues of the pharaohs often showed two snakes in the ruler's crown, not one. These snakes symbolized two Egyptian gods. The Roman poet Virgil agreed with Horace. Writing shortly after Cleopatra's death, he wrote of "the pair of asps in wait for her."[27]

The story of Cleopatra's death became generally accepted by writers, artists, and historians. During the Italian Renaissance (1400–1600), paintings showed a snake as the cause of Cleopatra's death. Other artists portrayed the same story during the eighteenth and nineteenth centuries. In his play *Antony and Cleopatra*, William Shakespeare wrote a famous death scene for Cleopatra. It was based on the story of the asp. According to Shakespeare, Cleopatra refused to go to Rome where she would be treated as "an Egyptian puppet. . . ." Cleopatra then directed one of her servants to:

> *Give me my robe, put on my crown;*
> *I have immortal longings in me: now no more*
> *The juice of Egypt's grape shall moist this lip. . . .*
> *[speaking to the asp]*
> *With thy sharp teeth this knot . . .*
> *Of life at once untie: poor venomous fool,*
> *Be angry, and dispatch.*
> *[Applying another asp to her arm]*
> *What should I stay." [Dies]*[28]

Shakespeare had Cleopatra killed by more than one asp in his play, just like Horace had in his poem. Whatever the true story, the death of Cleopatra at thirty-nine years of age became one of the most famous dramas in history. As Horace wrote: "She was no docile woman but truly scorned to be taken away in her enemy's ships."[29] Though she died relatively young, Cleopatra had lived as a proud, independent queen.

8

CLEOPATRA'S LEGACY

Although Cleopatra was defeated at Actium and died in 30 B.C., her memory did not fade. In fact, she became one of the most famous rulers in world history.

THE FATE OF CLEOPATRA'S EGYPT

Following the death of Cleopatra, Octavian ruled over Egypt. With Cleopatra's huge treasure, Octavian paid the soldiers who had helped him conquer Egypt. There was even enough left to give to the people of Rome. Octavian wanted to make sure that Antony was not remembered in Alexandria. Therefore, he had all of Antony's statues destroyed. Cleopatra's statues remained because one of her wealthy supporters, named Archibius, offered Octavian two thousand talents to preserve them.

Octavian did not plan to punish the Egyptians, even though they had supported Antony and Cleopatra. As Cassius Dio wrote:

> The truth was that he [Octavian] did not see fit to inflict any irreparable injury upon a people so numerous, who

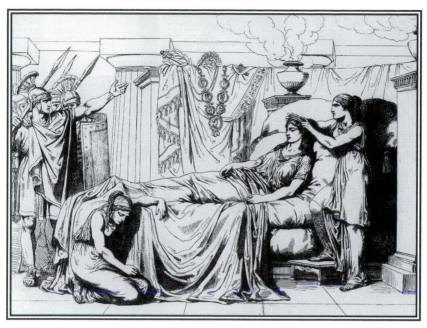

After the suicide of Cleopatra, Octavian (at left with arm raised) gained control over Egypt.

might prove very useful to the Romans in many ways. . . . The speech in which he proclaimed to them his pardon he delivered in Greek, so that they might understand him.[1]

Rome needed Egypt's huge wheat harvests. Indeed, Egypt exported approximately five million bushels of wheat to Rome each year. This was about one-third of what the Romans needed to feed their people in Italy.[2] In addition, Egypt exported other prized items, including beautiful glass products, jewelry made of gold, and papyrus. Well-to-do Romans also began having the walls of their homes painted with scenes of the Nile River and other parts of Egypt. In addition, they worshipped the Egyptian god Isis and made trips to her temples in Egypt.

Octavian did not punish the Egyptian people. However, he did not hesitate to help himself to some of Egypt's finest treasures. These included statues owned by the royal family and some of the wealthy citizens of Alexandria. In addition, Octavian took over the lands owned by the Egyptian priests. They became members of the Roman bureaucracy and were paid a salary by the government. Nevertheless, Octavian, like previous rulers, was seen as a god in Egypt. Like pharaohs in the past, Octavian was considered by the Egyptians to be a god living on earth. Temples were soon being built in Octavian's honor. And he was recognized as the heir of Alexander the Great. Octavian even established a new city called Necropolis, near Alexandria.

Octavian wanted to insure that new revolts would not break out in Egypt. Therefore, he needed to eliminate Caesarion—the son of Cleopatra and Caesar. Cleopatra had hoped to arrange Caesarion's escape to

ANTONY'S FATE

Although Cleopatra's statues were preserved, there were none that remained of Mark Antony. Octavian ordered that all of them should be destroyed. Indeed, the Roman Senate proclaimed that any images of Antony on coins should be removed. Roman parents were also forbidden to name their children Mark Antony, according to the historian Plutarch. While tearing down the statues of Antony, Octavian erected many new statues celebrating his victory at Actium.[3]

India. However, he was murdered along the way by agents of Octavian. Antyllus, Antony's son by his first wife Fulvia, was also executed. He was turned in to the Romans by his tutor, Theodorus, and he was decapitated. Octavian then went south along the Nile to Memphis, visiting much of Egypt. Like Egyptian kings before him, he wanted to be seen by the people. In this way, they would have little doubt that he was their new ruler.

CLEOPATRA'S INFLUENCE ON THE ROMAN EMPIRE

Octavian went back to Rome in 29 B.C. There he celebrated a great triumph that lasted for three days. It commemorated his victory at Actium and his conquest of Egypt. According to Cassius Dio, the celebration included "an effigy [statue] of the dead Cleopatra upon a couch . . . was carried by, so that in a way she, too, together with the other captives and with her children, Alexander, also called Helios [the sun], and Cleopatra, called also Selene [the moon], was a part of the spectacle and a trophy in the procession."[4] Antony and Cleopatra's two young children had been spared by Octavian and were brought to Rome. In fact, these small children were raised there by Antony's former wife, Octavia. Antony had divorced Octavia in 32 B.C. Eventually, Selene married King Juba of Numidia, located in North Africa. Historians are not certain what happened to Helios.

125

After his return to Rome, Octavian soon began to consolidate his own power over the Roman Empire. He never permitted himself to be called a dictator. Octavian had seen what happened to his great uncle Julius Caesar. Instead, he called himself *princeps*, meaning the leading man in Rome. His reign, therefore, became known as the Principate. Octavian also became known as Caesar Augustus. Although he did not call himself an emperor, he was the ruler of Rome and its empire, and thus the first Roman emperor.

Augustus rapidly reduced the size of the Senate, which had grown to one thousand men. Eventually, it contained only six hundred senators. Augustus consulted the Senate regularly as his advisors. He also appointed members of the Senate to govern Roman provinces. While keeping the Senate, however, Augustus turned it primarily into an advisory body. Its main role was simply to approve of decisions that Augustus had already made.

To do the actual work of governing the Roman Empire, Augustus created a large bureaucracy. It was loyal only to him. As historian Michael Foss has pointed out, it was similar to the "centralized Ptolemaic model,"[5] the one used by Cleopatra which Augustus had encountered when he entered Egypt. Although many provinces were governed by Roman senators, Augustus directly ran Egypt. It was annexed to the Roman Empire and governed by someone whom Augustus selected from his own staff. Augustus also required that the army swear an oath of loyalty to him. He personally appointed the top officers, so they would support him. He did not want the army supporting a general who might try to overthrow the government.

Among many Romans, Augustus was highly regarded. They considered him to be the man who brought peace to the empire following many years of civil war. In 2 B.C., he was given the title "Father of his Country." He also spent lavishly on adding new public buildings to Rome to increase the beauty of the city. Indeed, Augustus often claimed that "he found Rome a city of brick, and left it one of marble."[6] The building projects provided work for the poorer people of Rome.

The Augustan Age, as it was called, was a long period of peace. During this era, there was a great flowering of Roman literature. Among the foremost writers of the period were the poets Virgil and Horace.

NUMIDIA

Cleopatra and Antony's daughter Selene was made to marry King Juba II of Numidia by Octavian. The Kingdom of Numidia, located in present-day Algeria in North Africa, had a long relationship with the Roman Empire. Once part of the city-state of Carthage, the Numidians broke away in 206 B.C. and allied themselves with Rome and against Carthage in the Punic Wars. Later, King Juba I allied Numidia with Pompey against Julius Caesar. When Caesar was victorious, Numidia lost its independence and became part of the Roman Empire. Numidia once again was prosperous under Selene's husband King Juba II because he had gained the favor of Rome.

They wrote poetry about Cleopatra, among other subjects. Virgil also composed a great epic poem, known as the *Aeneid*. It was named after the Trojan hero Aeneas, who was considered the founder of Rome and is compared to the emperor Augustus in the poem. Meanwhile, Horace composed a series of poems, known as the *Odes*. The Roman poetry of the period often praised Augustus. By contrast, Cleopatra's life and her reign in Egypt received praise as well as criticism.

 ## VIEWS OF CLEOPATRA

For the next half-century after her death, Egyptians continued to honor Cleopatra. They referred to her simply as "the queen."[7] In Rome, the statue that Caesar had erected to Cleopatra was not removed. As late as the third century A.D., Cleopatra was worshipped as a goddess. She was considered by her followers as "the most illustrious and wise among women . . . great in herself and in her achievements in courage and strength."[8] Indeed, Caesar had regarded the Egyptian queen as a smart, capable leader.

However, other Romans felt differently. Cleopatra's image through much of history was developed in the years immediately after her death. Perhaps the most prominent in creating this image was Augustus himself. Formerly Octavian, he had defeated Antony and Cleopatra. According to historian Lucy Hughes-Hallett, he then "began to look around for a poet who could celebrate his talents and achievements in appropriately grand style."[9] Among them was the poet Horace. In one of his poems, Horace wrote of Cleopatra:

> . . . *A crazy queen was plotting . . . to demolish*
> *The Capitol and topple the Empire.*[10]

Another Roman poet who took up the cause against Cleopatra was Virgil. In his long poem the *Aeneid*, he described the story of the Trojan hero, Aeneas. On his long journey from Troy, Aeneas stopped in North Africa. There Dido, the queen of Carthage, tried to prevent Aeneas from leaving and win his love. But Aeneas did not stay and went on to Italy to found Rome. According to Lucy Hughes-Hallett, "No Roman alive when the poem was written could have read it without thinking of Cleopatra, of Julius Caesar who, 'duty-bound' like Aeneas, returned from Africa to Rome, and of Antony who did not."[11]

Indeed Cassius Dio reminded his readers that Mark Antony was "enslaved" by Cleopatra. As a result, Antony remained in the East, lived with the queen in Egypt, and took up her cause. He also battled Augustus for the future of the Roman Empire. The historian Plutarch agreed. He said that Cleopatra had "a thousand . . . sorts of flattery," designed to attract Antony.[12] The historian Florus, writing after Plutarch, added, "This Egyptian woman demanded from that drunken general the domination of Rome . . . and Antony promised it. . . . He forgot his nation, his name . . . and degenerated wholly into the style of that monster, in mind, in dress, in all his manner of life."[13]

Augustus was carrying out the duty of ruling the Roman world. Meanwhile, Plutarch pointed out that Antony and Cleopatra were busy enjoying lavish feasts in Alexandria. Plutarch mentioned that his grandfather had known someone who served at the court of Cleopatra. He described what this man saw at a feast for Antony and Cleopatra:

> So he was taken into the kitchen where he admired the ... variety of all things; but particularly seeing eight wild boars roasting whole, says he, "Surely you have a great number of guests." The cook laughed at his simplicity, and told him there were not above twelve to sup, but that every dish was to be served up just roasted to a turn, and if anything was just one minute ill-timed it was spoiled.[14]

Plutarch's story was designed to show how much food was wasted by Antony and Cleopatra.

The historian Pliny the Elder, writing in the first century A.D., described another extravagant banquet. This one was part of a contest between Antony and Cleopatra. They wanted to determine which one of them could put on the most lavish feast. During her banquet, Cleopatra took off an expensive pearl earring and dropped it into a cup of wine. Then she drank the wine and the pearl earring. The earring was worth thousands of dollars, but Cleopatra seemed to care nothing about wasting money.[15]

In short, the ancient Roman historians painted a very negative picture of Cleopatra. They believed that she lived a scandalous life in her relationships with Caesar and Mark Antony. The ancient historians also believed that Cleopatra was untrustworthy. While Antony gave her an empire, she was not loyal to him. Plutarch described the Battle of Actium as a seesaw contest that could have been won by Antony or Octavian. But just at the height of battle, Cleopatra suddenly decided to leave and set sail for Egypt. Plutarch implied that the queen picked the wrong time to leave the battle. When Antony went after her, Plutarch thought that the Roman commander had lost his ability to lead an army. "Here it was Antony showed to all the world that he was no longer . . . a commander or a man."[16]

Cassius Dio agreed with Plutarch's description of the battle of Actium. He said that Cleopatra "could not endure the long and anxious waiting until a decision could be reached, but true to her nature as a woman and an Egyptian, she . . . suddenly turned to flight herself and raised the signal for the others, her own subjects."[17]

Cassius Dio wrote that Cleopatra tried to flirt with Augustus when he later arrived in Alexandria just as she had done with Antony. Like Aeneas resisting Dido, Augustus successfully resisted the queen's charms. Instead, he performed his duty to Rome. Cassius Dio described Cleopatra this way:

> [She] was of insatiable [impossible to satisfy] passion and insatiable avarice [greed]; she was swayed often by laudable ambition, but often by overweening effrontery [great pride]. By love she gained the title of Queen of the Egyptians, and when she hoped by the same means to win also that of Queen of the Romans, she failed of this and lost the other besides. She captivated the two

greatest Romans of her day, and because of the third she destroyed herself.[18]

 ## CHAUCER'S VIEW

The English poet, Geoffrey Chaucer, presented a different portrait of Cleopatra. In his book *The Legend of Good Women*, written from 1385–1386, he described Cleopatra as a person committed to her love for Antony. Chaucer lived during the Age of Chivalry. European knights lived by a strict code of honor. A knight was expected to perform heroic deeds and dedicate them to a beautiful woman. These deeds were symbols of his love.

In turn the woman was expected to be faithful to her knight and dedicate herself to him. Chaucer portrayed the love between Antony and Cleopatra like the relationship between a knight and a noblewoman. As Chaucer wrote, "this noble queen . . . loved this knight, for his merit and his knighthood; and certainly, unless the books lie, he was of his person and nobility and . . . hardiness worthy of any . . . alive."

Chaucer added that Augustus was "maddened by this deed [the relationships between Antony and Cleopatra]," and started a war against them. When the war was lost, Antony committed suicide and Cleopatra followed him. As Chaucer put it, "she received her death cheerfully, for the love of Antony who was so dear to her. And this is truth of history, it is no fable."[19] According to Chaucer, Cleopatra died for love. Like some people in his era, Chaucer regarded her suicide as a noble act.

However, today we know that suicide is never the solution for any problem.

VIEWS OF CLEOPATRA IN THE RENAISSANCE

The negative images of Cleopatra continued during the European Renaissance (1400–1600). Cleopatra was portrayed as a lustful woman, who loved men without marrying them. Thus, she led a sinful life, opposed to the teachings of Christianity. In his book *Concerning Famous Women*, the fourteenth-century Italian writer Giovanni Boccaccio criticized Cleopatra for her behavior. "Cleopatra was an Egyptian woman who became an object of gossip for the whole world. . . . She gained glory for almost nothing else than her beauty, while on the other hand she became known throughout the world for her greed, cruelty, and lustfulness."[20]

Boccaccio reflected a popular view of women during the period. They were not known for rational thought, according to leading European writers. These writers believed that they were usually weak individuals. They needed to rely on men, whom they attracted with their beauty. Boccaccio emphasized that Cleopatra "easily ensnared that lustful man [Antony] with her beauty. . . . She kept him wretched in love with her."[21] Boccaccio also repeated the story, drawn from Pliny, of Cleopatra's lavish banquet.

A similar portrait was presented by the renaissance poet Petrarch, who criticized Julius Caesar, the great conqueror. He allowed himself to be conquered by love

This painting by Renaissance painter Michelangelo shows Cleopatra with two asps around her shoulders.

and Cleopatra. As Petrarch wrote, "in the midst of so many conquests he himself was conquered at Alexandria by princely love." As historian Mary Hamer wrote, "Love and humiliation for the warrior hero are inescapably linked."[22]

 ## MODERN VIEWS OF CLEOPATRA

The positive image of Cleopatra presented by Chaucer became more popular during the late nineteenth and early twentieth centuries. At this time, according to historian Mary Hamer, the roles of women were changing, as they gained more rights and worked outside the home. Instead of depending totally on their husbands, women became more independent. As Hamer wrote, the story of Cleopatra began to fascinate many women. They read about her courageously entering the palace, surrounded by her brother's army, and visiting Julius Caesar. Instead of adopting Augustus' view of Cleopatra, they began to agree with Caesar's opinion of her. As Hamer wrote, Augustus' view of Cleopatra "might not be the last word: Caesar may register surprise and alarm at the arrival of Cleopatra, but he is also intrigued. Despite himself, he takes pleasure in Cleopatra, in her refusal to be left out and in her courage."[23]

One historian, W.W. Tarn, wrote in the 1930s that there were only two leaders who had frightened Rome. One of them was Hannibal during the second century B.C. He had led the invasion by Carthage into Italy. The other leader, according to Tarn, was Cleopatra.[24]

Historian Michael Grant has called Cleopatra a "woman of single-minded determination . . . a ruler of outstanding ability and experience."[25] She had learned from her father how to preserve Egyptian independence by allying herself with Rome. That was her goal when she charmed and impressed Julius Caesar. Together with Caesar, she sailed south along the Nile on a huge, luxurious barge. This was designed to impress her subjects. As historian Lucy Hughes-Hallett wrote, she was an expert at propaganda. Instead of words, however, she used images. Since most of her subjects could not read, they would be impressed with "the language of drama and spectacle."[26]

When Antony called Cleopatra to Tarsus, she did not come immediately. Instead she waited until she was ready. Timing was everything, in her mind. When

PAINTINGS OF CLEOPATRA

Paintings of Cleopatra during the Renaissance period and later show her often dressed in lavish clothing. One of the popular subjects of paintings was Cleopatra's banquet where she supposedly drank the pearl. Painters also showed the meeting of Cleopatra and Antony at Tarsus. In these paintings, the queen's clothing included heavy silk gowns, furs, and expensive jewelry. Such clothing was worn by noble women in Europe during the Renaissance and later. Cleopatra herself would never have worn these heavy, warm clothes fifteen hundred years earlier in the hot Egyptian climate.

Cleopatra first met Antony, she made a grand entrance on a barge. Antony was struck by the grandeur of her giant boat. He was also impressed by the number of servants who accompanied her, and by Cleopatra herself. Cleopatra was dressed to resemble Venus. Later, she identified herself with the goddess Isis. Isis was worshipped throughout the Egyptian world. People believed that Isis could perform miracles and could give them protection from harm. Isis was the special guardian of women.

In 34 B.C., Cleopatra and Antony also appeared together during the Donations of Alexandria. Cleopatra was dressed as Isis, the ancient goddess of Egypt. With great pageantry, she and her children took back control of the large empire that had once belonged to the Ptolemies. But the spectacle of the Donations signified more than just a larger, more impressive empire. Cleopatra's son, Alexander Helios, also symbolized the dawning of a new age. In the past, Alexander the Great had hoped to unite the west and the east in a single empire. He wanted to be its ruler—Alexander of the Sun. At the Donations of Alexandria, Antony and Cleopatra made it clear that Alexander Helios was intended to take the place of Alexander the Great.[27]

In contrast to Augustus, Cleopatra and Antony had a broader view of empire. Antony saw himself ruling a Roman empire influenced by Greece and the nations of the east. These included Judea, Syria, Turkey, Persia, India, and Egypt. All of these areas had been brought together many centuries earlier by Alexander the Great. Through his conquests, he had spread Greek civilization eastward. There Greek culture had mingled with eastern cultures to form a new Hellenistic culture (Hellenistic means Greek). Antony imagined that he would rule this Hellenistic Empire with Cleopatra as his ally and coruler. Cleopatra believed the same thing. Many lands in the eastern Mediterranean might have welcomed a new empire ruled from Alexandria. Historian Lucy Hughes-Hallett wrote that the "Hellenistic peoples of the eastern Mediterranean were far from content as subjects to Rome: they were looking for a champion and a liberator."[28]

This empire might have been created if Antony and Cleopatra had won the Battle of Actium. But Augustus had no intention of letting an empire slip away from the grasp of Rome. He battled Antony and Cleopatra to safeguard the power and glory of Rome. Augustus had no interest in sharing power with anyone else, especially an empire based in Alexandria. Where Antony and Cleopatra had one vision of empire, Michael Grant wrote that "Augustus felt otherwise . . . he was ultimately the heir of Roman imperialism: the Italians were unmistakably intended to be top dogs."[29] At Actium, Augustus's view of the Roman Empire was victorious.

Other historians have talked about one of the great "what ifs" of history. What if Antony and Cleopatra had actually won the Battle of Actium? But as historian Jack Lindsay wrote, "Antony had no chance of winning after he became identified with the east." Octavian had the armies of Rome behind him. These were much more powerful than the forces that Antony and Cleopatra could put together. In addition, the Roman people

CLEOPATRA'S NEEDLES

Cleopatra's Needles are two tall obelisks—narrow stone monuments. Each obelisk is sixty-eight feet high and weighs one hundred and eighty tons. One of them is currently located in New York City in Central Park. The other is in London, at Westminster on the Victoria Embankment. Although they are called Cleopatra's Needles, they were actually produced much earlier. Historians believe that the obelisks were produced about 1500 B.C. by the pharaoh Thutmose III. The obelisks also contain words that were put on them to celebrate the victories of a later pharaoh, Rameses II. Each obelisk has four faces. On one face of the needle in New York, there is an inscription:

The Horus, Strong-Bull-Beloved-of-Ra
The King of Upper and Lower Egypt. . . .
Ra, created by the gods, who founded the Two
Lands, the Son of Ra,
Ramesses, Beloved-of-Amun.

backed Octavian. They did not want to be ruled by another power, especially one from the east.

Antony and Cleopatra were identified with the east. Cleopatra was a Greek. Antony, although a Roman, had become her husband and seemed to be under her control. The Romans saw the Greeks as their rivals and did not intend to be ruled by them. Instead, the Romans saw themselves as the new rulers of the Mediterranean. Octavian, not Cleopatra, was the leader that they intended to follow. While Octavian represented the future, Cleopatra seemed to symbolize the past. Therefore, her defeat seemed inevitable.

Nevertheless, Cleopatra may have done the best job possible with the resources she had in Egypt. The queen recognized that Rome was far more powerful than Egypt. Cleopatra also realized that she needed the Romans to keep Egypt independent. As historian Michael Foss wrote, "The most brilliant of all Cleopatra's deep political perceptions was the clear

Cleopatra's needle rises above the treetops in Central Park in New York City.

understanding that Egypt could never be saved from Rome except by a Roman."[30] What Cleopatra refused to accept was the fact that Rome would preserve the power of the Ptolemies. She could have remained alive and on the throne, Foss wrote, if she had bowed to the power of Rome. But Cleopatra refused.

Therefore, she became the leader of a glorious, but doomed, lost cause. As a great leader, Cleopatra is remembered as one of the foremost monarchs of history.

CHRONOLOGY

331 B.C.—Alexandria is founded.

304—Reign of Ptolemy Soter.
−282 B.C.

282—Ptolemy II, ruler of Egypt, expands empire.
−246 B.C.

246—Reign of Ptolemy III.
−221 B.C.

200—Decline of Egyptian power under Ptolemaic
−100 B.C. pharaohs.

80—Reign of Ptolemy Auletes, father of Cleopatra.
−51 B.C.

69 B.C.—Cleopatra is born.

51 B.C.—Cleopatra becomes Queen of Egypt.

49 B.C.—Cleopatra is driven off throne by her brother, Ptolemy XIII; Julius Caesar takes control of Rome.

48 B.C.—Julius Caesar defeats Pompey at Pharsalus; Julius Caesar enters Alexandria and starts love affair with Cleopatra.

47 B.C.—Julius Caesar defeats Ptolemy XIII; Cleopatra regains throne.

46 B.C.—Cleopatra arrives in Rome.

44 B.C.—Julius Caesar is assassinated; Cleopatra returns to Egypt.

43 B.C.—Formation of the Second Triumvirate.

42 B.C.—Julius Caesar's assassins are defeated at Philippi by Mark Antony.

40 B.C.—Mark Antony and Cleopatra travel to Alexandria; Cleopatra gives birth to twins.

37 B.C.—Mark Antony and Octavian renew Second Triumvirate.

36 B.C.—Mark Antony invades Parthia, but his army is defeated.

34 B.C.—Donations of Alexandria increase Cleopatra's empire.

32 B.C.—Octavian declares war on Cleopatra.

31 B.C.—Octavian defeats Mark Antony and Cleopatra at Actium.

30 B.C.—Octavian enters Alexandria; Mark Antony and Cleopatra die.

CHAPTER NOTES

CHAPTER 1. TRIUMPH

1. Cassius Dio, *Roman History*, Book 42, October 21, 2003, <http://penelope.uchicago.edu/Thayer/E/Roman/Texts/Cassius_Dio/42*.html> (April 7, 2005).

2. *Plutarch's Lives* (New York: Random House, 1955), p. 883.

3. Ernle Bradford, *Julius Caesar: The Pursuit of Power* (New York: Morrow, 1984), p. 226.

4. *Plutarch's Lives*, pp. 883, 1119.

5. Cassius Dio, *Roman History*, Book 42.

6. Michael Grant, *Cleopatra* (New York: Simon and Schuster, 1972), p. 65.

CHAPTER 2. CHILDHOOD

1. Michael Foss, *The Search for Cleopatra* (New York: Arcade Publishing, 1997), p. 36.

2. Ibid., p. 36.

3. *Plutarch's Lives* (New York: Random House, 1955), p. 1119.

4. "Athaneus (fl. c. 200 CE): The Great Spectacle and Procession of Ptolemy II Philadelphus, 285 BCE," *Ancient*

History Sourcebook, May 1998, <http://www.fordham.edu/halsall/ancient/285ptolemyII.html> (April 7, 2005).

5. John Boardman, et al., eds., *The Oxford History of the Classical World* (New York: Oxford University Press, 1987), p. 339.

6. Ibid., p. 341.

7. Foss, pp. 63–64.

8. Susan Walker and Peter Higgs, eds., *Cleopatra of Egypt: From History to Myth* (Princeton, N.J.: Princeton University Press, 2001), p. 19.

9. Foss, p. 61.

10. Walker and Higgs, p. 20.

11. Edith Flamarion, *Cleopatra: The Life and Death of a Pharaoh* (New York: Abrams, 1997), p. 26.

12. Michael Grant, *Cleopatra* (New York: Simon and Schuster, 1972), p. 15.

CHAPTER 3. CLEOPATRA'S EGYPT

1. Michel Chauveau, *Egypt in the Age of Cleopatra* (Ithaca, N.Y.: Cornell University Press, 1997), p. 55.

2. Susan Walker and Peter Higgs, eds., *Cleopatra of Egypt: From History to Myth* (Princeton, N.J.: Princeton University Press, 2001), p. 133.

3. Sarah B. Pomeroy, *Women in Hellenistic Egypt* (New York: Shocken Books, 1984), p. 57.

4. Ibid., p. 148.

5. Chauveau, pp. 88–90.

6. Michel Chauveau, *Cleopatra: Beyond The Myth* (Ithaca, N.Y.: Cornell University Press, 2000), p. 6.

7. Michael Foss, *The Search for Cleopatra* (New York: Arcade Publishing, 1997), p. 17.

8. Chauveau, *Egypt in the Age of Cleopatra*, p. 73.

9. Gunther Holbl, *History of the Ptolemaic Empire* (London: Routledge, 2001), p. 59.

10. Chauveau, *Egypt in the Age of Cleopatra*, p. 189.

11. Foss, pp. 16–17.

12. Michael Grant, *Cleopatra* (New York: Simon and Schuster, 1972), p. 49.

13. Ibid., pp. 53–54.

CHAPTER 4. CLEOPATRA AND ROME

1. *Plutarch's Lives* (New York: Random House, 1955), pp. 755–756.

2. Ernle Bradford, *Julius Caesar: The Pursuit of Power* (New York: William Morrow, 1984), p. 22.

3. Ibid., pp. 35–36.

4. *Plutarch's Lives,* p. 856.

5. Suzanne Cross, "Youth to Consulate," *Julius Caesar, The Last Dictator*, March 19, 2005, <http://heraklia.fws1.com/early_life/index.html> (March 22, 2005).

6. Bradford, pp. 49–50.

7. Ibid., p. 874.

8. John Leach, *Pompey the Great* (London: Rowman and Littlefield, 1978), p. 184.

9. *Plutarch's Lives*, p. 785.

10. Leach, pp. 202–206.

11. Edith Flamarion, *Cleopatra: The Life and Death of a Pharaoh* (New York, Abrams, 1997), p. 40.

CHAPTER 5. CLEOPATRA, PTOLEMY, AND CAESAR

1. Edith Flamarion, *Cleopatra: The Life and Death of a Pharaoh* (New York, Abrams, 1997), p. 40.

2. *Plutarch's Lives* (New York: Random House, 1955), p. 883.

3. Flamarion, p. 125.

4. Arthur Kahn, *The Education of Julius Caesar* (New York: Schocken Books, 1986), p. 369.

5. Cassius Dio, *Roman History*, Book 42, October 21, 2003, <http://penelope.uchicago.edu/Thayer/E/Roman/Texts/Cassius_Dio/42*.html> (April 7, 2005).

6. Julius Caesar, "The Alexandrian Wars," *Caesar's Commentaries on the Gallic and Civil Wars*, Electronic Text Center, University of Virginia Library, n.d., <http://etext.lib.virginia.edu/etcbin/toccer-new2?id=CaeComm.sgm&images=images/modeng&data=/texts/english/modeng/parsed&tag=public&part=3&division=div1> (March 22, 2005).

7. Cassius Dio, *Roman History*, Book 42.

8. Michel Chauveau, *Cleopatra: Beyond The Myth* (Ithaca, N.Y.: Cornell University Press, 2000), p. 30.

9. Jack Lindsay, *Cleopatra* (New York: Coward MacCann and Geoghegan, 1970), p. 108.

CHAPTER 6. THE REIGN OF CLEOPATRA

1. Flavius Josephus, "Antiquities of the Jews: Book XV—From the Death of Antigonus to the Finishing of the Temple by Herod," *Works of Flavius Josephus*, trans. William Whiston, n.d., <http://www.ccel.org/j/josephus/works/ant-15.htm> (March 22, 2005).

2. Michael Grant, *Cleopatra* (New York: Simon and Schuster, 1972), p. 98.

3. Eleanor Goltz Huzar, *Mark Antony, A Biography* (Minneapolis: University of Minnesota Press, 1978), p. 23.

4. Ibid., p. 127.

5. Grant, pp. 95–97.

6. Ibid.

7. *Plutarch's Lives* (New York: Random House, 1955), pp. 1118–1119.

8. Grant, p. 121.

9. *Plutarch's Lives*, p. 1120.

10. "Antony by Plutarch," *The Internet Classics Archive*, n.d., <classics.mit.edu/Plutarch/antony.html> (April 7, 2005).

11. Huzar, p. 155.

12. Paul Halsall, "Suetonius: The Divine Augustus," *Internet Ancient History Sourcebook*, October 1998, <http://www.fordham.edu/halsall/ancient/suetonius-augustus.html> (March 22, 2005).

13. Josephus, *Works of Flavius Josephus.*

14. Mary Hamer, *Signs of Cleopatra* (London: Routledge, 1993), p. 9.

15. Jack Lindsay, *Cleopatra* (New York: Coward MacCann and Geoghegan, 1970), pp. 271–272.

16. Michael Foss, *The Search for Cleopatra* (New York: Arcade Publishing, 1997), p. 130.

17. *Plutarch's Lives*, p. 1129.

18. Grant, p. 148.

19. Ibid., p. 149.

20. Ibid., p. 153.

21. Susan Walker and Peter Higgs, eds., *Cleopatra of Egypt: From History to Myth* (Princeton, N.J.: Princeton University Press, 2001), p. 142.

22. Michel Chauveau, *Cleopatra: Beyond The Myth* (Ithaca, N.Y.: Cornell University Press, 2000), p. 56.

23. *Plutarch's Lives*, p. 1134.

24. Lindsay, p. 280.

CHAPTER 7. A DECISION AT ACTIUM

1. Susan Walker and Peter Higgs, eds., *Cleopatra of Egypt: From History to Myth* (Princeton, N.J.: Princeton University Press, 2001), p. 195; Michael Grant, *Cleopatra* (New York: Simon and Schuster, 1972), p. 188.

2. Michael Grant, *Cleopatra* (New York: Simon & Schuster, 1972), p. 201.

3. Ibid., pp. 193–194.

4. Edith Flamarion, *Cleopatra: The Life and Death of a Pharaoh* (New York, Abrams, 1997), pp. 78–79.

5. Eleanor Goltz Huzar, *Mark Antony, A Biography* (Minneapolis: University of Minnesota Press, 1978), p. 211.

6. *Plutarch's Lives* (New York: Random House, 1955), p. 1137.

7. Huzar, p. 215.

8. Cassius Dio, *Roman History,* Book 50, July 25, 2003, <http://penelope.uchicago.edu/Thayer/E/Roman/Texts/Cassius_Dio/50*.html> (April 7, 2005).

9. Ibid.

10. Jack Lindsay, *Cleopatra* (New York: Coward MacCann and Geoghegan, 1970), p. 342.

11. *Plutarch's Lives*, p. 1138.

12. Huzar, pp. 219–220.

13. *Plutarch's Lives*, p. 1142.

14. Grant, p. 214.

15. Huzar, p. 221.

16. Flavius Josephus, "Antiquities of the Jews: Book XV—From the Death of Antigonus to the Finishing of the Temple by Herod," *Works of Flavius Josephus*, trans. William Whiston, n.d., <http://www.ccel.org/j/josephus/works/ant-15.htm> (March 22, 2005).

17. Lindsay, p. 411.

18. Flamarion, pp. 88–89.

19. Huzar, pp. 223–224.

20. *Plutarch's Lives*, p. 1146.

21. Ibid., p. 1147.

22. Grant, p. 225.

23. Cassius Dio, *Roman History*, Book 50.

24. *Plutarch's Lives*, pp. 1151–1152.

25. Ibid.

26. Michael Foss, *The Search for Cleopatra* (New York: Arcade Publishing, 1997), p. 175.

27. Grant, p. 227.

28. William Shakespeare, *The Complete Works of Shakespeare* (New York: Cumberland Publishing, 1911), pp. 1171, 1173.

29. Flamarion, p. 114.

Chapter 8. Cleopatra's Legacy

1. Cassius Dio, *Roman History*, Book 51, August 30, 2003, <http://penelope.uchicago.edu/Thayer/E/Roman/Texts/Cassius_Dio/51*.html> (April 7, 2005).

2. Michael Foss, *The Search for Cleopatra* (New York: Arcade Publishing, 1997), p. 181.

3. Jack Lindsay, *Cleopatra* (New York: Coward, MacCann and Geoghegan, 1970), pp. 442–443.

4. Cassius Dio, *Roman History*, Book 51.

5. Foss, p. 183.

6. Paul Halsall, "Suetonius: The Divine Augustus," *Internet Ancient History Sourcebook*, October 1998, <http://www.fordham.edu/halsall/ancient/suetonius-augustus.html> (March 22, 2005).

7. Michael Grant, *Cleopatra* (New York: Simon and Schuster, 1972), p. 233.

8. Lucy Hughes-Hallett, *Cleopatra: Histories, Dreams and Distortions* (New York: Harper and Row, 1990), p. 70.

9. Ibid., p. 59.

10. Edith Flamarion, *Cleopatra: The Life and Death of a Pharaoh* (New York, Abrams, 1997), p. 114.

11. Hughes-Hallett, p. 61.

12. *Plutarch's Lives* (New York: Random House, 1955), p. 1120.

13. Susan Walker and Peter Higgs, eds., *Cleopatra of Egypt: From History to Myth* (Princeton, N.J.: Princeton University Press, 2001), p. 300.

14. *Plutarch's Lives*, p. 1120.

15. Walker and Higgs, p. 305.

16. *Plutarch's Lives*, pp. 1141–1142.

17. Cassius Dio, *Roman History*, Book 50, July 25, 2003, <http://penelope.uchicago.edu/Thayer/E/Roman/Texts/Cassius_Dio/50*.html> (April 7, 2005).

18. Cassius Dio, *Roman History*, Book 51.

19. Mary Hamer, *Signs of Cleopatra* (London: Routledge, 1993), pp. 132–133.

20. Walker and Higgs, p. 302

21. Edith Flamarion, p. 129.

22. Hamer, p. 39.

23. Walker and Higgs, p. 309.

24. Hamer, p. 110.

25. Grant, p. 237.

26. Hughes-Hallett, p. 75.

27. Ibid., p. 100.

28. Ibid., p. 91.

29. Grant, p. 235.

30. Foss, p. 185.

GLOSSARY

ARTISAN—A craftsperson.

ASP—A poisonous snake.

CAVALRY—Soldiers on horses.

CENTURION—A Roman officer who commanded a group of about eighty men.

CLERUCHS—Greek soldiers who farmed plots of land in Egypt.

COHORT—A Roman military unit consisting of one thousand men.

COLONNADE—A row of columns that usually supports a roof.

CONSUL—Roman leader of government.

DIOKETES—Minister of finance in the Egyptian government.

DRACHMA—Unit of money in Greece and the ancient world; six thousand drachmas equal a talent.

HEPTASTADIUM—Long man-made causeway that connects Alexandria with Pharos.

IRRIGATION—The process of channeling water to lands that do not have it.

LEGION—A unit of six thousand men in the Roman army.

MUMMIFICATION—The process of preserving a dead body.

MUSEUM OF ALEXANDRIA—House of the Muses—a center of learning in Alexandria.

NOMOI—Government administration districts in Egypt.

PHARAOH—King of Egypt.

PHAROS—Island near Alexandria containing Pharos Lighthouse, also called the Great Lighthouse.

PRINCIPATE—The name that Octavian gave to his government.

STRATEGOS—Administrators of the nomoi.

TALENT—Unit of money in Greece and the ancient world, equivalent to fifty-seven pounds of silver.

TRIBUTARY—A smaller river or stream that branches off a larger river.

FURTHER READING

Adams, Michelle Medlock. *The Life and Times of Cleopatra*. Hockessin, Del.: Mitchell Lane Publishers, 2005.

Bergin, Mark. *Warfare in the Ancient World*. Columbus, Ohio: Peter Bedrick Books, 2003.

Califf, David J. *Battle of Actium*. Philadelphia: Chelsea House Publishers, 2004.

Cumming, David. *The Nile*. Milwaukee, Wis.: World Almanac Library, 2003.

Gaff, Jackie. *Ancient Egypt*. Chicago, Ill.: Heinemann Library, 2005.

Jeffrey, Gary and Anita Ganeri. *Cleopatra: The Life of an Egyptian Queen*. New York. Rosen Publishing Group, 2005.

Kaplan, Leslie. *Primary Sources of Ancient Civilizations: Egypt.* Powerkids Press, 2004.

MacDonald, Fiona. *Cleopatra: Queen of the Kings*. London: Dorling Kindersley, 2003.

Millard, Anne. *Going to War in Ancient Egypt*. London: Franklin Watts, 2004.

Morris, Neil. *Everyday Life in Ancient Egypt*. Mankato, Minn.: Smart Apple Media, 2003.

Nardo, Don. *Cleopatra*. San Diego, Calif.: Lucent Books, 2005.

————, ed. *Living in Ancient Egypt*. San Diego, Calif.: Greenhaven Press, 2004.

————. *A Travel Guide to Ancient Alexandria*. San Diego, Calif.: Lucent Books, 2003.

Reid, Struan. *The Life and World of Cleopatra*. Oxford, England: Heinemann Library, 2003.

Trumble, Kelly. *The Library of Alexandria*. New York: Clarion Books, 2003.

Winters, Kay. *Voices of Ancient Egypt*. Washington, D.C.: National Geographic, 2003.

INTERNET ADDRESSES

EGYPTOLOGY ONLINE
Every aspect of ancient Egyptian history and daily life.
<http://www.egyptology.com>

THE FIELD MUSEUM, CLEOPATRA EXHIBITION
<http://www.fieldmuseum.org>
Click on "Exhibits" in the right-hand column. Click on "Past Exhibits" in the right-hand column. Scroll down and select "Cleopatra Exhibition Website."

THE HOUSE OF PTOLEMY
Resources on the Egypt of Cleopatra and the other Ptolemies.
<http://www.houseofptolemy.org>

INDEX